Library Patrons' Privacy

Library Patrons' Privacy

Questions and Answers

Sandra J. Valenti, Brady D. Lund,
and Matthew A. Beckstrom

 LIBRARIES
UNLIMITED®

An Imprint of ABC-CLIO, LLC

Santa Barbara, California • Denver, Colorado

Library of Congress Cataloging-in-Publication Data

Names: Valenti, Sandra J., author. | Lund, Brady, 1994- author. |
    Beckstrom, Matthew, author.
Title: Library patrons' privacy : questions and answers / Sandra J.
    Valenti, Brady D. Lund, and Matthew A. Beckstrom.
Description: First edition. | Santa Barbara, California : Libraries
    Unlimited, [2022] | Includes bibliographical references and index.
Identifiers: LCCN 2021016460 (print) | LCCN 2021016461 (ebook) |
    ISBN 9781440874109 (paperback ; acid-free paper) | ISBN 9781440874116 (ebook)
Subjects: LCSH: Library legislation—United States. | Data protection—Law
    and legislation—United States. | Library records—Law and
    legislation—United States. | Internet access for library users—Law
    and legislation—United States. | Library users—Legal status, laws,
    etc.—United States.
Classification: LCC KF4319.P75 V35 2022 (print) | LCC KF4319.P75 (ebook) |
    DDC 342.7308/58—dc23
LC record available at https://lccn.loc.gov/2021016460
LC ebook record available at https://lccn.loc.gov/2021016461

ISBN: 978-1-4408-7410-9 (paperback)
        978-1-4408-7411-6 (ebook)

25 24 23 22 21   1 2 3 4 5

This book is also available as an eBook.

Libraries Unlimited
An Imprint of ABC-CLIO, LLC

ABC-CLIO, LLC
147 Castilian Drive
Santa Barbara, California 93117
www.abc-clio.com

This book is printed on acid-free paper ∞

Manufactured in the United States of America

For my husband, Dale, whose unfailing support has helped me overspend on electronics for decades.
—Sandra J. Valenti

I am appreciative to everyone who supports the tremendous opportunities I have to learn and contribute to the library profession and library and information science research.
—Brady D. Lund

I would like to dedicate this book to all the libraries and librarians fighting every day to protect the privacy of every library user. I have to thank my coauthors, who really did the lion's share of the work for this book and for their support. Of course, none of this would be possible without the love and support of my amazing wife. Thank you!
—Matthew A. Beckstrom

Contents

Acknowledgments

We would like to acknowledge the contributions of the reviewers and editors of this book for helping to see it come to fruition. Thank you!

Introduction

The Importance of Evidence-Based Practice in Information Policy

Hello reader! Welcome to this discussion of some of the biggest ethical crises in information privacy faced by library patrons today. You may be wondering, what sets this book apart from other library privacy books available today? Simple. This is not a book that tells you "this is what we say is best and you must do it." Rather, it is a book written with a firm belief in evidence-based practice, the idea that professionals should stay abreast of current research and trends in practice in order to inform best practice at their own institutions. Evidence-based practice first emerged in the medical professions, where it was decided that research, personal wisdom, and insight about a specific situation was more likely to result in positive medical outcomes than tradition and personal convictions.

Following this belief in evidence-based practice, this book synthesizes librarian opinions, library policies, case studies, empirical research for library and information science and other fields, American Library Association publications, privacy philosophy . . . and a bit of our own opinions, developed while reading all this literature. This book does not say "this is definitely the answer for your library"; it says, "this is what researcher X said, library Y did effectively, and the ALA suggests." We all know that if you have worked at one library, then . . . you have worked at one library. Unless you want to pay for us to personally visit your library and solve all its privacy problems based on its unique status and needs (which we are more than happy to do), this is the next best thing. Each chapter of this book is a complete review and analysis of a different library privacy issue. As the book progresses, we introduce increasingly more complex technologies and issues.

Why focus on privacy? Librarians consistently regard privacy as an incredibly pressing concern (Zimmer 2014).[1] The evolution of technology and attacks against privacy is rapid, and many professionals are unable to keep on top of these trends. Privacy policy is also an area that is particularly amenable to evidence-based practice. We can see what a library's policy is, and we can also see how well that policy works. If an idea works for dozens of libraries of different type (public, academic, corporate), then it is easy to argue that it will work for your library as well. Information privacy is also a highly interdisciplinary concern, which takes concepts from the information sciences and applies them to libraries—this is a concept that appeals to the authors' interests and to library and information science researchers. Most importantly, we think the topic is pressing and insufficiently discussed in the literature and implemented in practice, so we want to highlight and hopefully help to remedy this situation.

THE PURPOSE OF POLICY

Policy is a major focus of this book, as policy both defines library actions and protects the library from attacks by those who may wish to undermine its decision-making authority. Policy is often developed by a committee. At public libraries, this is typically the library board—a group of elected or appointed volunteers who take part in the governance of the library. At academic libraries, this is often a committee comprised of library and college/university leadership. Policy is developed to set a precedent, to provide something to look to, rather than make up decisions on the spot. Like this book, policy is something physical that you can point to as justification for your actions (and with any luck, this book will be influential enough to inform some library policies). Policy allows libraries to divert attention from the library employees to an inanimate object, the policy and library board/governance committee. Like with a theoretical framework used in research, a policy makes logical order of where the library's rules originate and why.

Policy, however, is not the sole focus of this book. There are, in fact, many cases in which policy cannot accurately anticipate how an incident will unfold, or where the level of ambiguity in a situation cannot be captured or explained in a written statement. It is in these cases that this book draws on narratives from those who have experienced this type of situation, or on ethical conceptions that provide some guidance on how to respond.

By the way, if you do discover some policies in this book that you would like to use in your library, we are sure that the library from which the policy originates would be glad to let you use them, but please do ask for permission first! After all, all website content is copyrighted, so if you use it you will either need to attribute it to the creator (as we do in this book) or ask for permission to use the copyrighted content. Do not simply copy a policy from another library's website and say "okay, done!" We are sure that you readers know this, but consider it a legal disclaimer on our part (akin to a "do not steal jewelry" disclaimer in a book about excellent jewels from around the world).

THE ORGANIZATION OF THIS BOOK

The book is divided into three parts, each with a slightly different theme and tone. Part I focuses on physical and virtual items owned, loaned, or representing patrons. In Chapter 1, we focus on the loss of physical items such as flash drives, notebooks, wallets, and laptops, and whether it is appropriate to check these items for personal identifying information. We also discuss library computer logouts and whether it is appropriate to log out a computer when it is abandoned by a patron. In Chapter 2, we look at the issue of privacy and confidentiality for patron records and also discuss the prospect of the anonymous checkout and elimination of patron records altogether. Chapter 3 discusses photography and video recording within the library and questions like "should patrons be permitted to take photos of library facilities, employees, or other patrons?" There is also a special section on social media policy in libraries. Finally, Chapter 4 focuses on when an incident escalates and law enforcement must be called on to intervene.

Part II of the book discusses basic computer privacy practices and their implications for library policy. In Chapter 5, we examine basic threats to library patrons' data privacy, including both physical (another patron spying over one's shoulder) and virtual (collection of data from websites). Chapter 6 discusses privacy challenges provoked by the need to work or access library resources remotely, as occurred during the 2020 COVID-19 pandemic. During this time, privacy policy was frequently overlooked—but we contend that it should not have been!

Finally, Part III of the book discusses the current status and future of general information privacy challenges and opportunities and speculates on the roles that libraries will need to take in continuing to support patron privacy. Chapter 7 takes a more up-close perspective on some of the topics touched on in Chapter 5, discussing the extent of data tracking and theft and what emerging roles information professionals may want to take in stemming the growth of these privacy invasions. Chapter 8 describes how connecting to a public computer network can threaten one's own devices as well as those of a library or other organization, and what roles professionals can take in ensuring these networks are secure. Lastly, Chapter 9 discusses the dark web, a topic that draws a lot of interest among librarians and privacy experts alike, but has yet to be offered as a fundamental privacy service in most libraries in the United States.

The chapters in each part of the book are organized somewhat uniquely in order to reflect the complexity of the technologies, policies, and challenges faced and the practical organizational (Chapters 1–6) versus more forward-focused (Chapters 7–9) topics. Though the chapters progress in term of technological complexity, all of the challenges discussed throughout the book pose significant ethical quandaries. This book serves as a reference and unbegrudging guide to these complex threats, with the aim of better informing both your knowledge of information privacy and library privacy policies and practices.

Join us as we investigate your biggest questions about library patron privacy.

NOTE

1. Michael Zimmer, Librarians' attitudes regarding information and Internet privacy, *Library Quarterly: Information, Community, Policy* 84, no. 2 (2014): 123–151.

PART I

Getting Our Boots on the Ground: The Dirty Work of Patron Privacy

The invasions of privacy that are most likely to work their way onto the radar of library patrons are relatively "small" things: what do I do with this flash drive I found? Is a check-out system that requires me to use a card with my name on it really private? Can I take pictures of interesting things I see in the library? What do I do when I see two people arguing in a hallway? These are not massive technological challenges; they may be duties that are frequently consigned to nonprofessional library staff. Yet these challenges are incredibly important to the way in which the service quality of your library is perceived. They are concerns that deserve to be directly addressed in every library's policy.

ONE

Missing/Unattended Items in the Library

John is the circulation desk manager at a large, urban public library in the upper Midwest. Along with overseeing the work of 14 part-time circulation desk assistants, John is responsible for monitoring the library spaces around the circulation area, which includes a workstation with 10 public-use computer terminals. One day, as John walks past these computers, he notices a USB flash drive (we are going to call it this, because that's the name Microsoft gave it, but you might also refer to it as a thumb drive, pen drive, memory stick, etc.) in an unattended computer. No one has used that particular terminal for several hours, and there is no way to track which patrons used the computer last.

John suspects that if he were to open the files in the flash drive, one of them would contain information that could help identify the patron who left it behind. However, he is reluctant to open a flash drive when he has not been given permission to do so by its owner. Instead, he places the drive in the circulation desk's lost-and-found box (which is only accessible to circulation desk employees).

Several weeks later, a patron arrives at the circulation desk and says that she lost her flash drive a week ago and has been looking for it ever since. She does not think it is likely, but perhaps she left it here at the library? John asks the patron what computer she believes she was using during her previous visit, and she indicates that it was the same computer in which John found the flash drive. It fits the scene, it fits the timeline, but John still cannot be sure that the flash drive is hers. He debates whether he should ask the patron what files are on the drive so that he can check if it is hers, but doubts that this is any better than opening the files to search for identifying information.

What should John do? Is there any way to get this flash drive to its owner without infringing on the owner's privacy? Could the best solution be to destroy the flash drive altogether? Situations like John's are faced by library employees every day. Whether it is a flash drive, a backpack, a notebook, laptop, or cell phone, the problem at its core is the same: should we as information professionals infringe on the privacy of patrons to mitigate loss or preserve privacy at all costs?

Unfortunately, John's troubles were not done. Later that day, he happens across a computer that is logged into a patron's account but is left unattended by that patron. How should he proceed? Should he ignore it, expecting that the patron will soon return while opening the risk that the patron's privacy could be compromised? Or should he log out of the account at the risk of irritating the patron? In both the case of the flash drive and the computer login, John only wants what is best for the patron—the problem is that he does not know what the best thing is for that patron, especially when he does not even know which patron is the rightful owner/user.

In our first chapter, let's explore the situations John is facing. We will look to what the American Library Association has to say about patron privacy, see how librarians are currently navigating these challenges, and look at some theoretical perspectives from library and information science and beyond.

A LONG-STANDING EPIDEMIC OF LIBRARIES EVERYWHERE

If you have ever worked in a library in any role for any period of time, you are sure to have faced some situation similar to John. Ethical quandaries like John's are among the most common topics of discussion on library listservs (a major inspiration for this book). In fact, in an informal survey conducted on February 12, 2019, on the Library and Information Technology Association (LITA) listserv, respondents reported discovering an object that might potentially contain personal information (like a flash drive) four to six times per week on average.

Some of the objects found in a library's areas lack any personal information (or personal identifying information, like an owner's name), such as physical items: headphones, books, coffee mugs, and water bottles. Some of these items are quite humorous, such as those items reported in the lost and found at Bates College in Maine:

- Course notebook with notes on Platonic concepts of beauty: Is it universal ideal, or is it localized in the eye of the beholder?

- "First Visit to Disneyland" pin

- Luggage tag with no name
- Plastic bag with mandala-style designs
- Empty orthodontic appliance case
- Response card clicker, used by students to answer class questions in real time
- Perfect fit button, allows wearer to adjust their pants waist
- A few rings
- Single knitted glove
- Single KB-brand sock[1]

These are not the items we are particularly interested in for this discussion (though if the rings have monetary value, we may change our tune a bit). We are interested in the cases where the personal information of the patron is at risk. What if John opened a document on the flash drive he found, looking for the patron's name, and happened on the patron's entire five-year tax history, social security number, and contact information? Even if John is a completely upstanding, trustworthy individual, this is a major breach of the patron's privacy. If you were in the position of the patron and knew that a library employee had seen that personal information, would you ever want to visit that library again?

This is why these topics are so hotly debated. This is not a discussion about whether you should hold onto the single used sock you found or throw it away; it is potentially the privacy and security of information that, if it reached the wrong hands, could completely ruin a life. It is potentially the same information that medical professionals have to go through extensive training in order to handle and can be banned from the profession for ever breaching its confidentiality. Yet we do not know whether this is the case (it is unlikely that an individual would carry a flash drive with all this information into a public library, but not impossible) or if it is simply a single Word document with a class assignment (but even in this case, whether privacy should be infringed by the library is highly controversial).

Here's an example from the news headlines. In 2008, a UK-based information technology periodical, *The Register*, reported two incidents, occurring in 2006 and 2008, where Dutch military and NATO intelligence information was left on a USB flash drive in a public library (in the Netherlands and Sweden, respectively).[2] This information was discovered by a librarian, who had accessed the content of the flash drives to look for an owner only to find vital government secrets. If libraries have policy that allows for flash drives to be opened and explored by an employee, they are potentially entrusting them to responsibly handle military intelligence. There has to be a lot of faith to entrust the responsible handling of information that is likely worth a tidy sum if delivered to the wrong hands, or that a rogue librarian does not pull an Edward Snowden (personal views aside, that probably is not the best move for the future funding of a public or federal library). That is an extreme case, of course, but one that is not completely improbable. It is equally possible that a lost notebook, an unlocked cell phone, or a computer logged into a patron's email account could contain sensitive information.

WHAT DO THE PRACTICING LIBRARIANS SAY?

Let's return to that informal survey of the LITA listserv for a moment. There were only two questions on the survey, the first being how many objects with personal information do you find each week, and the second being what do you do with those objects. The answers to the second question are quite revealing. The most frequent response (n=30/66, 45 percent) is that they open files on the flash drive/skim through the notebook/etc. to try and identify the owner. Fifteen (23 percent) say that they hold onto the object until someone comes and claims it (with the primary validation of ownership being the description of the object). Fifteen (23 percent) respondents admit that no universal policy is in place, so the answer varies from employee to employee. Yet others offer their own unique solutions to identifying the owner (more on that in a little bit). None say that they destroy the object. There is no clear preferred method for handling this situation. None of the strategies are used by 50 percent or more of the respondents. The correct procedure is, indeed, quite hazy.

Most of the popular informal library/librarian blogs and Twitter accounts appear to hold the belief that searching through the lost item for contact information is the right way to go.[3] Those patrons that have their lost flash drives returned by a librarian who searched its files generally seem happy to have their drive returned and unconcerned about privacy concerns, at least among those who share their experiences on social media. Perhaps if no one is complaining, we should simply maintain the status quo?

Some libraries have made their suggestions and procedures known through their websites and social media. One example is the University of Missouri. They offer two important tips specifically in regard to the USB drive:

1. Add a contact folder to your USB drive which contains your name and email so we know it belongs to you.

2. Encrypt the most important files on your drive so nobody can steal your information if you do lose it.[4]

These tips hint that the policy at Missouri is to open the flash drive files and search for identifying information. Their suggestion to do so while maintaining privacy, however, is unique. By advising patrons to encrypt important files and add a clearly named document that contains just the patron's contact information, the library can identify the owner without invading their privacy too much (beyond the titles of documents). The only problem with this policy is that it puts the impetus on the patron to take the time to encrypt their files and add a document with contact information. This is not common practice, so it becomes the duty of the library to try and educate all patrons about the need to take these steps. If a patron does not take these steps and the flash drive is left behind, the library is back to searching through all the files to try to find identifying information.

Fairmont State University in West Virginia offers a similar suggestion to Missouri in regard to cell phones. Fairmont suggests using your name written on a plain-colored background as the lock screen wallpaper so that the library can identify the phone's owner.[5] Of course, this means that anyone who gets their hands on your phone will now have your name, which itself raises some privacy concerns.

How about computer log-outs? There are three major camps (these will be discussed in more detail in the policy section). The first is to set automatic log-out timers on the computers. The second is to have a policy in place that clearly states that after x number of minutes, a library employee will log out the computer and make it available to any other library patron for use (this is often done less for privacy concerns than for "computer hogging" concerns). The final camp is to do nothing; if a patron leaves a computer unattended, that is on them.

WHAT DOES LIBRARY POLICY SAY?

Existing library policies pertaining to objects potentially containing personal information vary. Some libraries have policies that clearly have not been updated in well over a decade (the mention of floppy disks is a big indicator).

LA Law Library has a clear and detailed policy: "Flash drives in the lost-and-found may be viewed on public PC by Staff for identification purposes. Patron must provide reasonable identification of the drive (e.g., contents, description or location) before flash drive may be claimed," and other items with personal information "may be searched for contact information to facilitate notifying the owner. Patron must provide reasonable identification of the item (e.g., background picture, password, description and/or location) before the device will be released."[6]

Madison Public Library in Lake County, Ohio, has the policy that, "Flash drives left in the library will be held for 14 days. Due to patron privacy library staff will not access data saved on flash drives to determine ownership. After 14 days, flash drives will be wiped and discarded."[7] Williamsburg Libraries, in Massachusetts, has the policy that, "Flash drives left in the library will be held for 30 days. Due to patron privacy library staff will not access data saved on flash drives to determine ownership. After 30 days, flash drives will be destroyed and discarded."[8]

These policies return us to the "other" category of the survey of the LITA listserv. The majority of "other" responses were some variation of these combined policies. "For the first x number of days, we will hold on to the flash drive and you may claim it simply by describing the drive and where you left it. After x days, the flash drive will be wiped/destroyed." Fourteen days is a very common length of time for flash drives to be held onto before they are wiped.

The Library of Congress turns all found items to the U.S. Capitol Police, headquartered in the Madison Building.[9] All items are held (not searched) for 60 days before being disposed of. At Harvard and Yale University, all items of perceived value are forwarded to the campus police for handling.[10] This removes the responsibility for the personal information stored within items from the library and puts it in the hands of individuals trained to work with personal information in a confidential manner.

As mentioned in the prior section, policy falls into three camps (or two camps of policy and one camp of the absence of policy). The first camp, where a computer will auto-logout after a period of time, is probably the most common. It is captured in official library policy, such as at Southern Methodist University's Libraries: "for security reasons a warning pops up that auto logoff will occur after 5 minutes of inactivity."[11] The other common library policy is to allow a library employee (like John in our example) to log out a computer if it is left unattended for a period of time. For MacOdrum Library at Carleton University in Ontario, a warning is given after a computer is observed to be unattended for five minutes via an "unattended workstation form."[12] After 10 minutes, they will follow a standardized procedure to log out the computer:

- Check if the absent student is at the printer or close by
- If not, an IT Help Desk staff member will go to the unattended workstation along with a full time staff member from the CCS Service Desk (room 509) or one of the full time staff from Research Help
- They will save all work to the network drive (G or U) using FILE / SAVE AS with filenames Unattended_temp_date
- They will then log the student off
- If there are any personal belongings left at the workstation they will be moved over to the Library Services Desk
- The next student in line will be allowed to use the computer[13]

The final common library policy is the absence of a policy. In such a case, a library may either a) have personal policy that varies from employee to employee, or b) consistently practice nonenforcement of any policy, meaning that a patron can leave the workstation unattended and logged in for an indefinite period of time. Anecdotally, it appears that this absence of policy is more common among smaller libraries (regardless of library type), while larger libraries seem to have one of the two above policies in place.

WHAT DOES THE ALA SAY?

The American Library Association's *Questions and Answers on Privacy and Confidentiality* and *Privacy: An Interpretation of the Library Bill of Rights* expand on the professional value of privacy by providing specific interpretations and guidance.[14] Neither document directly addresses flash drives, cell phones, or any other specific item that may contain personal information; however, both documents address personally identifiable information and the rights of library patrons. What follows is an interpretation of an interpretation of the library bill of rights pertaining to objects with personal and personally identifiable information and computer logouts.

What Should Be Our Expectation of the Patrons' Expectations Regarding These Items?

These documents clearly suggest that librarians should expect that patrons see them as another government bureaucrat or university official and be suspicious of librarians' motives. Librarians are trained and work hard to be perceived as individuals that deserve no suspicion or animosity, but the nature of the stereotyped traditional librarian and the nature of the government/university-employed position will also lend an aura of mistrust. The American Library Association suggests that strong, clearly stated, and consistently enforced policies both build trust with patrons and diminish the likelihood of improper handling of an ambiguous ethical situation.[15] In regard to items that potentially contain personal information, this can clearly be interpreted to mean that a policy should most definitely be in place for how to handle these items. The case of the 23 percent of respondents to the LITA survey who stated that they have no policy in place should be corrected. Perhaps such policy would not be so specific as naming flash drives but would refer to all special items that could contain personal information (cell phones, notebooks, contents of backpacks, laptops, etc.); these items should all be treated differently from a water bottle, hair brush, or old sock.

What Is the Best Policy?

Though it is clear a policy should be in place to ensure consistency and diminish improper handling of these materials, there is no clear indication of what the policy should be. There is contradictory evidence as to whether these items should be searched for contact information, left alone, or destroyed. The ALA policy does seem to indicate that library employees (particularly librarians) have some right to push the bounds of absolute privacy when necessary for the greater good. CIPA and other legislation also direct libraries to infringe on some rights of privacy and choice. So viewing the content of personal items may be permissible, given a consistently enforced policy (though this does not necessarily mean that it is the best policy). Other policies (namely, not viewing the contents of the item under any circumstances) are also permissible. All of these policies have some ethical, privacy, and practical implications that are not ideal.

For computer logouts, again a policy should definitely be in place. As long as a policy is in place and consistently enforced, it reduces complaints on the part of patrons frustrated that their work has been interrupted. It seems that the ALA guidelines may indicate a preference for the automatic logouts, as these are less evasive and mean that no employee will see the patron's documents. The downside to this policy is that if a computer logs out without saving documents, you will assuredly have some frustrated, even angry, patrons on your hands at times.

WHAT DO OTHER FIELDS SAY?

Here is a librarian's take on what an IT person would tell you to do if you found a flash drive and did not know who the owner was: bring it to IT! As fairly tech-savvy librarians, we would be reluctant to say that an IT person could do any better job than us (especially at making ethical judgments), but perhaps we are wrong in that belief? If we take a look at a convenient sample of the top-100 *U.S. News and World Report*–ranked universities and at the 2019 bachelor's and master's curriculum for information technology programs, we find that 96 percent of the programs offer a required or elective course in privacy or information ethics.[16] Conversely, among U.S.-based ALA-accredited Master of Library and Information Science programs, only 51 percent offer a similar course in privacy or information ethics. Perhaps IT administrators are better prepared to handle technology that potentially contains personal information of a patron? The obvious problem with such a belief is that many libraries are not staffed with a dedicated IT professional with an information technology/computer science/information systems degree.

There is a good reason why IT might advise you not to insert the flash drive into your computer: you really do not know what could be on it. Flash drives can be made to contain malicious components/software that could fry your computer or allow an external attacker to access information stored on the library's computer system. Opening files from a flash drive comes with the same risks as opening suspicious attachments on an email message. Of course, it does not necessarily make sense for this policy to be enforced for all lost items containing personal information—it does not make much sense to bring a lost backpack to IT for them to handle. In dividing up your lost and found, you just make the situation more confusing for the patron.

Let's look at other service industries to see what solutions they have created for working with lost personal items.

In general, it appears that the health professions treat patients' lost items with the same level of privacy as is expected of patient medical records. That means that it is not uncommon for the individual who discovered the item to search it for personal identifying information of the owner, with the assumption that any information discovered would be held to the same standards as medical information.[17] This policy aligns with what most respondents in the LITA listserv survey said about current library policy, though library professionals do not have the same level of universal ethical/privacy standards as medical professionals.

The general policy for the airline industry/Transportation Security Administration is to list where the item was found in as much detail as possible (e.g., "on the floor beneath seat 12C"), the time at which it was discovered (e.g., "10:32 a.m. after arriving in Kansas City on Flight 612BL, Northsouth Airlines"), and the details of the item's appearance (e.g., "black phone with green case and sunset screensaver"). The owner of the phone will then have to match their description of what, where, and when they lost closely to the details provided on this list. It is generally not the policy to seek out the owner unless the items are clearly labeled with contact information—if the item is important to the individual, they will have the impetus to retrieve it. Any items that potentially contain personal information are wiped/destroyed after 30 days.[18] Generally, all lost-and-found items are held in one location within the airport (in the case of the library, they might be held at the circulation desk—which is common practice now anyways—rather than at the desk of whomever discovered the item).

In hospitality (hotel) services, what to do with lost items with personal information is a fairly common discussion. Similar to a library, hospitality services generally have employees with varying levels of educational attainment, ranging from high school graduates or lower, up to individuals with master's degrees or above, depending on the specific institution. Ethics and privacy is discussed in the major hospitality management textbooks and housekeeping training manuals.[19] These materials do not seem particularly concerned with the idea of exploring items to identify personal information, though, generally, it is more common for the institution to simply have a lost and found and wait for the guest to come to them and describe the item.

Technically, according to the order of the law in most jurisdictions in the United States and around the world, lost property of value (which probably does not include any items we are discussing here—except maybe a wallet containing personal documents) should be turned in to a government official. Generally, after a period ranging from a couple of years to over a decade, the lost item becomes the property of the government (this is technically what the Library of Congress's policy is—after 60 days, the lost item becomes the property of the U.S. government and is usually disposed of).[20]

WHAT DO RESEARCHERS SAY?

We can begin by talking about what research suggests that we want to do when we find a flash drive sitting around without an owner: open it. A 2016 study at the University of Illinois discusses a project wherein the researchers dropped 297 flash drives across the university campus.[21] The vast majority of these flash drives were picked up and quickly plugged into a computer and their files opened. It turns out that people cannot resist knowing what interesting nuggets of information they have happened on. The researchers were interested in understanding information-seeking behavior pertaining to content on found flash drives to anticipate how a damaging computer attack could be conducted using these devices. This research indicates that individuals on a university campus are curious and inclined to open and search the flash drive—this also makes you wonder how many flash drives that are lost are picked up and pried into by other patrons, never to even see the lost and found. Of course, because we are inclined to do something in our nature does not at all mean that it is the right thing to do. In fact, often the opposite is true. Does the fact that we are naturally inquisitive and prying indicate that we should not be trusted to responsibly sift through personal items for contact information?

Libraries should consider how the ambiguity and inconsistency in privacy policies among libraries worldwide will impact how patrons perceive the viewing of content on their personal item by a library employee. Especially with emerging library technology, privacy concerns have been high and policy inconsistent.[22] We might not consider a flash drive an emerging library technology, but it is certainly one that comes with the same level of risks and—unlike many emerging technologies—also has physical threats to its privacy (i.e., theft of the drive). Beyond infringing on the privacy of personal information, a personal item in the hands of an irresponsible employee or patron could lead to a loss/theft of intellectual property.[23]

Are librarians legally permitted to destroy an item they discover in the library? For an item generally considered to be inconsequential should it be destroyed (even if this is not, in fact, the case), you are probably okay to destroy it if this falls in line with your policy. However, there is technically a legal gray area, as mentioned in the discussion of the "order of the law" above. Since most librarians can technically be viewed as government officials, it appears the answer would be yes, at least after a set period of time has passed. It is likely, however, that if a patron could prove the item was in the possession of the library and was immediately destroyed, there could be some repercussions (but it is not particularly plausible).

Again, if we look at studies of human behavior, we find an impetus for enforcing automatic computer logouts. Privacy is one of the most desired and least respected rights of humanity.[24] People never want their privacy infringed on but love to infringe on the privacy of others.[25] The anger a patron expresses for having their work lost is preferable to the anger a patron expresses for having their personal records, bank information, or intellectual property stolen (though studies suggest that in the short term, patrons may not see it this way—e.g., the privacy paradox).[26] Ethical and information science theory clearly suggest that a policy of auto-logout is ideal.

PHILOSOPHY OF PRIVACY AND PRACTICE OF LIBRARIES

Jeroen Van Den Hoven and John Weckert present a strong overview of moral philosophy as it pertains to information technology.[27] The authors discuss Norbert Wiener's (1894–1964) theories of information ethics as they pertain to modern human–computer interaction and information technologies. In information ethics, there is a conflict between the "ideal" and the "practical" (as there is in virtually all discussions of ethics). Information technologies are an enigma because they present both great opportunity and great risk. The ideal in the situation of the lost personal item is to preserve privacy at all costs, because library and information science has aligned with the ethical stance of privacy, which historically is an absolute philosophical stance with respect to information technology.[28] However, when this ideal is translated to practice, it means that the best solution for libraries is to destroy any lost item that might potentially contain personal information, because there is no way to ensure the item is definitely returned to its rightful owner without compromising privacy to some extent. Those who interpret the ethics of the profession as absolutes will be inclined to follow this ideal. This practice, informed by the philosophical ideal, however, likely conflicts with other ideals of service, access, preservation, and social responsibility. The ideals of these values would suggest that librarians should do everything in their power to return the item to its rightful owner and that destroying the item could do unrepairable damage to the owner (e.g., if there are valuable documents and the only copy of them is on the flash drive the library recovered).

To summarize the philosophy above, if you think philosophy and core values can tell you what to do, you are almost assuredly wrong. As with most philosophy (politics, religion, etc.), it is your interpretation of conflicting philosophies that will guide your decision. There are no guidelines in the ALA Core Values or information ethics that will give you a clear, conflict-free plan for handling items with personal information. Don't get it twisted; philosophy is valuable, but you must use it to guide decision-making, not allow it to make decisions for you.

The problem of computer logouts is a bit more straightforward. Having an auto-logout for the public computers in your library certainly appears to be the preferable solution. In this case, no one has access to the patron's information (as opposed to when an employee logs the computer out or the computer is just left unattended). The challenge that might occur is when a patron berates you and your fellow employees because they lost their work, but on the scale of ethical crises, angry patron pales in comparison to breach of privacy.

WHAT DO WE SAY?

We may not be able to provide a definitive answer of what you should do, but there are certainly indications of best practice. The first thing every library should do is have a policy in place. With full clarity and authority, we can say that having a policy for found items that potentially contain personal information is very important, and this policy should be distinct from a general lost-and-found policy. Not all found objects are the same, just like not all emails, phone calls, personal conversations, and library documents are the same. Certain objects must be treated with a greater level of privacy and security than others.

There is reason to suggest that opening the flash drive/item and skimming through the files is likely not the best policy or, at least, should be done by a very trustworthy (probably MLIS-credentialed) employee. Information is a valuable commodity. Would you want just any random individual to sift through your wallet with your credit card numbers and driver's license inside it? If there is something valuable, the library should expect that the patron will come and hope to claim the item quickly. Perhaps waiting several days to make sure the patron will not claim the item based on the description, before invading that patron's privacy by searching the item for personal information, is preferable. Furthermore, there is always a risk of an electronic appliance, like a flash drive, causing harm to library equipment. While the likelihood of this occurring is low, if it should happen it could cause disastrous and costly effects.

There is also very clear indication that putting the item in a lost-and-found box and then allowing any person to come along and sift through the box is not a good policy. This is straightforward. It is simply too easy for a patron to "find" something that is not theirs if they are allowed to see what is there. Having the patron describe the item (ideally in as much detail as possible, using the airline strategy of what, where, and when) is preferable. Again, in most cases these items will have no consequential information, but some will. The same standards apply to library documents and the expectation of employees not to share these documents outside of the work environment. Few of these documents would have major consequences if made public, but that a) does not mean that they should be made public, and b) does not mean that a few of these documents would have major consequences (even if it is unforeseen). When an item with personal/private information is in the possession of the library, it is the library's job to hold the item with the same level of responsibility and security that it would any other of its possessions.

As mentioned in the prior section, the solution to computer logouts is fairly straightforward. Virtually all evidence points to having automatic logouts after a set period of inactivity. This policy will likely be annoying to patrons, especially when it is first enforced, but there is no ALA core value of not annoying patrons. The only argument that could reasonably be made as to why libraries should not have automatic logouts in place is the preservation of knowledge. Ultimately, in the case of both computer logouts and lost items containing personal information, there must be some responsibility on the part of the patron to save their documents and put their name on their items; otherwise the result when one of their items is lost or left unattended may be less than ideal. Libraries have the duty to inform patrons of both policy and measures to reduce privacy infringement/loss of work.

CONCLUSION

Congratulations! You have just finished reading the longest discussion of the library's lost and found ever written. We hope that we have shown that having such a discussion about some of these items (probably not the sock or the half-empty bag of chips) is important. The implications of who discovers these items and what they do with them could potentially be damaging to a patron. The items should really be treated as an extension of the individual, and we, as library employees, should afford the same level of privacy and confidentiality to these items as we would to the individual regardless of what the procedure is for reuniting the individual and their property. The same goes for computer logouts—privacy should be prioritized over the fear of confrontation from an angry patron. Most importantly, this chapter highlights the imperative of having strong and detailed policy for your library. As long as a policy is in place, it serves as a barrier to protect you and your library from backlash and guide procedure and decision-making.

This chapter is level one on the scale of controversial topics. Consider it a warm-up. In the following chapters, we will dig into major ethical crises that pose immediate threat to libraries and their patrons. Join us as we move deeper into the ethical questions we all face on a daily basis as library and information professionals.

NOTES

1. Jay Burns, *Here are the 23 items in the library's lost and found on November 13, 2018*, retrieved November 15, 2018. https://www.bates.edu/news/2018/11/15/whats-in-the-ladd-library-lost-found-on-nov-13-2018/

2. Jan Libbenga, "Nato secrets USB stick lost in Swedish library," *The Register*, retrieved March 4, 2019. https://www.theregister.co.uk/2008/01/04/another_stick_with_military_secrets_found/

3. Brian Herzog, *Lost and found flash drives*, retrieved July 4, 2019. http://www.swissarmylibrarian.net/2012/01/24/lost-and-found-flash-drives/

4. Noel Kopriva, *PSA: Remember your USB flash drives!*, retrieved April 7, 2019. https://library.missouri.edu/news/engineering-library/psa-remember-your-usb-flash-drives

5. Kelly Bradish, *How do I put my name on my phone's lock screen?*, retrieved June 12, 2019. http://ask.library.fairmontstate.edu/faq/85114

6. Los Angeles Law Library, *Lost-and-found,* retrieved July 2, 2019. https://www.lalawlibrary.org/about-us/lost-and-found

7. Madison Public Library Board of Trustees, *Lost and found policy,* retrieved June 20, 2019. https://www.madison-library.info/lost-and-found-policy/

8. Williamsburg Public Libraries, *Williamsburg Libraries lost & found policy*, retrieved July 1, 2020. https://www.meekins-library.org/ckfinder/userfiles/files/Lost%20%26%20Found%20Policy%20approved7172017.pdf

9. United States Library of Congress, *Theft or loss of property*, retrieved July 8, 2020. https://www.loc.gov/rr/main/inforeas/theft.html

10. Harvard University Police Department, *Lost and found*, retrieved January 21, 2019. https://www.hupd.harvard.edu/lost-and-found; Yale University, *Lost & found*, retrieved January 21, 2019. https://your.yale.edu/community/public-safety/campus-safety-services/lost-found

11. Southern Methodist University Libraries, *How do I stop a computer from auto log-off*, February 1, 2019. https://askus.smu.edu/faq/153813

12. Carleton University MacOdrum Library, *Unattended workstation policy*, retrieved February 12, 2019. https://library.carleton.ca/about/policies/unattended-workstation-policy

13. Ibid.

14. American Library Association, *Privacy: An interpretation of the library bill of rights*, retrieved March 1, 2019. http://www.ala.org/advocacy/intfreedom/librarybill/interpretations/privacy; American Library Association, *Questions and answers on privacy and confidentiality*, retrieved March 2, 2019. http://www.ala.org/advocacy/privacy/FAQ

15. Ibid.

16. U.S. News and World Report, Best Online Master's in Information Technology Programs, retrieved April 17, 2021. https://www.usnews.com/education/online-education/computer-information-technology/rankings

17. Kansas University Medical Center, *A. R. Dykes Library*, retrieved August 7, 2019. https://library.kumc.edu/

18. Transportation Security Administration, *Lost & found*, retrieved January 14, 2019. https://www.tsa.gov/contact/lost-and-found

19. John R. Walker and Josielyn T. Walker, *Introduction to hospitality management* (Upper Saddle River, NJ: Prentice Hall, 2004); Sudhir Andrews, *Hotel housekeeping: A training manual* (New York, NY: McGraw-Hill Education, 2013).

20. Cornell University Legal Information Institute, *Lost property*, retrieved January 16, 2019. https://www.law.cornell.edu/wex/lost_property

21. Matthew Tischer, Zakir Durumeric, Sam Foster, Sunny Duan, Alec Mori, Elie Bursztein, and Michael Bailey, "Users really do plug in USB drives they find," *Proceedings of the 2016 IEEE Symposium on Security and Privacy*. https://ieeexplore.ieee.org/abstract/document/7546509/authors#authors

22. Bobbi Newman and Bonnie Tijerina, *Protecting patron privacy* (Lanham, MD: Rowman and Littlefield, 2017); Michael Zimmer and Kenneth Blacks, "Assessing the treatment of patron privacy in library 2.0 literature," *Proceedings of the 2012 iConference*, pp. 501–503. 2012.

23. William M. Landes and Richard A. Posner, *The economic structure of intellectual property law* (Cambridge, MA: Harvard University Press, 2009); Richard A. Spinello, "Intellectual property rights," *Library Hi Tech* 25, no. 1 (2007): 12–22.

24. William A. Parent, "Recent work on the concept of privacy," *American Philosophical Quarterly* 20, no. 4 (1983): 341–355.

25. F. Schoeman, "Gossip and privacy," In R. F. Goodman and A. Ben-Ze'ev (Eds.), *Good gossip*, 72–84 (Lawrence: University Press of Kansas, 1994).

26. Grace Ng-Kruelle, Paul A. Swatman, Douglas S. Rebne, and J. Felix Hampe, "The price of convenience: Privacy and mobile commerce," *Quarterly Journal of Electronic Commerce* 3 (2002): 273–286.

27. Jeroen Van Den Hoven and John Weckert, *Information technology and moral philosophy* (Cambridge, UK: Cambridge University Press, 2008).

28. Ibid.

TWO

Patron Records and the Anonymous Checkout

Emily is the director of a midsize suburban library. She heads a staff of four full-time (MLS) librarians and 12 full-time and part-time (non-MLS) library staff serving in a range of specialized departments. The area of town where the library is located has traditionally been considered to have low crime; however, two years ago, the local dog food plant closed, leaving hundreds out of work, which soon resulted in a spike in blue-collar crime in the neighborhood. During the past two years, the library has worked to bring in career coaches, offer resume assistance, and provide spaces for satellite courses for a nearby community college. This has led to the library becoming a hotspot for the local police, who suspect that many of the criminals are likely the same unemployed workers attending these opportunities.

One evening, following a library board meeting, the local chief of police approaches Emily. He notes the uptick in crime and the users of the library and suggests that they may be able to curb some of the illegal activity in the city if they had access to some library records, such as who is attending these opportunities offered by the library, what books these patrons are checking out, and their browsing behavior on the library's computers. While he says that he cannot make her do it, he strongly advises that she comply and provide the information.

The following morning, Emily calls an emergency meeting for all library employees. She describes her experience with the police chief and asks what the staff believes should be done. The staff have very mixed feelings. Some individuals, who have been victims of the uptick in crime, believe that anything that could be done to decrease the crime rate should be done with no hesitation. One of the librarians on staff strongly opposes providing this information, appealing to the American Library Association's core values of privacy and confidentiality. Others, whose families have been direct victims of the closing of the plant, say it is inhumane to treat these individuals who are seeking to improve themselves and find employment as though they are all criminals because a few (maybe) are engaging in illegal activity.

Given the heterogeneity of the responses, Emily decides it is best to bring the public into these discussions as well. However, on the evening of the public forum, two groups of protestors, on both sides of the issue, get into a conflict on library property that results in several injuries. The police chief immediately calls Emily and says this whole mess has gone too far and she must give up the patron data immediately. She does not know if she can hold off these requests any longer, fearing for the safety and well-being of her library and herself.

A CLASH OF VALUES

The point of the example above is not to suggest that police and librarians are always adversaries. Generally, both parties have the same goal of creating informed and peaceful members of a democracy. However, these situations do happen, because the information that libraries collect about patron information behavior can be highly valuable for predicting behavior outside of the library. Criminal offenders are only one example. This information would also be valuable to publishers and booksellers who could direct-market a new book to a library patron based on similar books they check out at the library— and many more. The ethical crisis at the core of these situations is whether we value privacy and confidentiality over the utilization of this information to potentially benefit society.

As you might expect, this is a crisis that often pits the core values of librarianship (privacy and confidentiality) against the personal morals of the library employee (anything to stop crime). It is also a crisis that is by no means new. As noted by Stacey Bowers (2006) (whose article "Privacy and Library Records" is highly recommended as further reading), challenges to the privacy of patrons' records date back nearly to the foundation of libraries themselves, with noted legal precedence on this topic as early as the late nineteenth century (with foundations in the Constitution of the United States). In 2007, Trina Magi reported that Vermont library directors estimated receiving over 1,200 requests for patron information over a one-year period.[1]

As noted by James Comey (yes, that James Comey) in an article about the USA PATRIOT Act and confidentiality of information, sometimes collecting patron information in libraries brings about results, such as the case of a New York-based al-Qaeda recruit who was using the library's Internet to email associates overseas and coordinate activities.[2] However, proponents of confidentiality in library and information organizations would argue that these cases are infrequent, and, regardless, it is not legal or ethical to collect information about citizens without their knowledge or consent.[3] This is a core provision of the silent oath librarians take when entering the profession.

We are not here to say carte blanche that ALA core values should supersede personal morals. That both a) is a cheap answer to a complex situation, and b) endows a level of power to the American Library Association that it may or may not actually deserve. Rather, we will take the same approach as in the prior chapter to spell out how different individuals, organizations, and schools of thought address this question, offer what our position would be, and invite you to consider these arguments to inform your own decision-making process.

THE ANONYMOUS CHECKOUT

One strategy to eliminate the possibility of data surveillance is to create an anonymous system for patron records. Presently, there is no perfect and consistent way to accomplish this end; however, blockchain has been suggested as a means to achieve anonymity and security in library records and services.[4]

Blockchain is a public ledger or database that displays a history or genealogy of transactions.[5] In the most basic sense, blockchain need not necessarily be a computerized system and can be created as a manual ledger of transaction history.[6] "Blocks" are packages of information about new transactions that are added to a "chain" of previous blocks. Users (and even nonusers) of a blockchain can access the chain's ledger and track the history of a block as part of the larger chain. The blockchain system is inherently transparent, and this builds necessary trust in the system.[7]

A blockchain transaction looks like that pictured in Figure 2.1. The first number in the sequence is the transaction identifier (hash). The second number is the date and time the transaction was submitted. The third number is the pseudonymous identifier of the individual initiating the transaction (in

7c3219edfe8c07937fd0a30793db50618fb234dcf6be353c3c7834698a2e58a3
2018-06-16 00:06:18 1KTvaF3MtZav9WAGJYMJtABkaJebNYkwza → 3Mm8A4Y
GZN4tyHpgMsV3k1fopxsrzo2sR5 0.00172 BTC

Figure 2.1   Example of a Blockchain Transaction

this case sending an amount of Bitcoin to the other user). The fourth number is the pseudonymous identifier of the individual receiving the transaction. The final number is the product of transaction: 0.00172 BTC transferred from the initiator to the recipient.

While this may seem to be a jumbled mass of characters, on the users' end it actually looks no different than a banking account on their phones. Users have a "virtual wallet" that contains an individual's owned blocks (in the case of Bitcoin, these are the "coins" themselves—just pieces of code like above). Ownership of blocks can be readily exchanged using QR codes created by one phone and scanned by another. If a virtual currency was associated with a book, patrons could use a virtual wallet to scan books and have the virtual ownership transferred to their accounts during the period of use before exchanging the ownership back to the library. In this case, patrons could remain anonymous, while the library would still be able to dictate which people could lend materials (as administrators of the blockchain system, they could dictate who can have a pseudonymous identifier) and keep track of which materials are currently on loan.

The important lesson to gather from the above example is that blockchain preserves privacy by assigning pseudonyms for user accounts.[8] In the case of using library materials, this would mean that individuals lending materials that some might consider inappropriate (e.g., a teenager in a politically conservative municipality looking up information about homosexuality) could lend the materials without there being any record for community members or public services librarians to reveal the true identity of the individual.

Blockchain, however, is not without its limitations. The biggest limitation is cost. Maintaining a blockchain system is expensive (energy costs alone would likely price out most libraries) and requires highly trained individuals (which most libraries, unfortunately, would likely not be able to afford to employ). Such a system, given current limitations in blockchain design, would also rely on patrons being fully trustworthy (i.e., it would be a lot easier to steal items since it takes time for the system to validate a transaction as opposed to a traditional automated library system that can update transactions nearly instantaneously).

At present, the anonymous checkout is not practical, so how can we navigate the problem Emily is facing given current practical options?

WHAT DO PRACTICING LIBRARIANS SAY?

Stacey Bowers makes an important point about the legitimacy of using patron records to make judgments about an individual's character or behaviors.[9] The idea that materials a patron lends/reads indicates anything about that patron's motivations is untenable. For instance, there are innumerable reasons why a patron might check out a book on white supremacy that have nothing to do with supporting personal beliefs in favor of a bigoted perspective, such as improving general knowledge (perhaps for the magnanimous goal of preventing history from repeating itself) or simply a morbid curiosity that will not translate to any change in beliefs or practices (such as when one watches television shows about serial killers). Given this fact, it is a bit easier to defend your library (though by no means a *breeze*) from unauthorized requests to collect patron records (i.e., the library director has less of a task to convince library employees that the records should not be shared). This is why the example to kick off this chapter did not involve looking at what materials were used by patrons but rather who are the patrons themselves. In this example, it is very likely that sharing the records of who is using the library will indeed identify some of the individuals who are committing crimes.

Many real libraries have faced similar situations to that of Emily and the employees, and directors of these libraries can provide important guidance. One example is the "Connecticut Four," whose story was discussed in a 2016 article published in *American Libraries*. The Connecticut Four were a group of four board members of a Connecticut library consortium who were faced in 2005 with a request from the Federal Bureau of Investigation (FBI) to provide all patron lending and Internet use records in the preceding year to help identify potential criminal offenders/national security threats.[10] Under the threat of criminal prosecution, the Connecticut Four denied the request and filed a lawsuit challenging it. With the support of the American Civil Liberties Union (ACLU), the Connecticut Four got the FBI to withdraw its request. This, of course, is not the ideal situation for your library to face, but it does set a precedent that your library should be aware of: that requests for patron records can be successfully challenged. Libraries should not be put in the position where they feel left without any recourse other than to do what is demanded of them.

South Central Library System in Madison, Wisconsin, provides thorough advice to libraries on preparing for police requests for patron records.[11] Developed by practicing librarians for practicing librarians, the guide leads libraries through the entire process of developing a plan, meeting with stakeholders, and executing the plan. Cornell University has a procedure in place for its employees to follow when patron information is requested, which may be useful for librarians facing requests of their own.[12] There are many other libraries in the United States that offer similar guidance (simply conduct a Google search). The consistent theme is that libraries, and especially frontline library employees, should have a plan before the request arrives.

In Jean Preer's 2008 book *Library Ethics* (which is one inspiration for this book), she dedicates a chapter to confidentiality of patron information, wherein she reiterates what the library systems above encourage, "librarians must make sure that the library has in place proper policies, approved by the library board, to protect patron privacy, and that all library employees and volunteers understand the right to privacy and are prepared to defend it."[13] Preer also indicates that facing a challenge to this policy will likely not be easy. Not all people believe privacy should be a protected right, and, indeed, it was not even accepted by society at large as a right until well into the twentieth century. Nonetheless, having an approved policy in place compels employees to do as directed in the policy, ensuring that challenges do not overwhelm the employee into providing the information and instead get redirected to library administration, who may work with legal counsel to develop an appropriate response.

WHAT DOES LIBRARY POLICY SAY?

Library policies vary based on the states in which they are located. The American Library Association provides a list of state privacy laws regarding library records at http://www.ala.org/advocacy/privacy/statelaws. In most states, the law will be some variation of this statute, which comes from the State of Kansas:

> Except to the extent disclosure is otherwise required by law, a public agency shall not be required to disclose . . .
>
> (23) Library patron and circulation records which pertain to identifiable individuals.[14]

However, some states have laws that are more or less restrictive, such as California, which has a specific state code for library patron record privacy:

> All patron use records of any library which is in whole or in part supported by public funds shall remain confidential and shall not be disclosed by a public agency, or private actor that maintains or stores patron use records on behalf of a public agency, to any person, local agency, or state agency except as follows:
>
> (a) By a person acting within the scope of his or her duties within the administration of the library.
>
> (b) By a person authorized, in writing, by the individual to whom the records pertain, to inspect the records.
>
> (c) By order of the appropriate superior court.[15]

In this case, it is very clear that only with a court warrant can any individual not authorized by the patron or employed by the library (with bona fide reason) access a patron's record. In this case, it is clear that the police chief cannot force Emily to provide the patron records, unless a specific crime has occurred, the police have credible evidence that suggests that the patron record is vital to the investigation, and the approval of the court is received. Saying that it "might help track down criminals" if you could see the records is simply not enough and could result in unlawful seizure should the police take the records without permission. While Emily may face social pressures, she should not face any legal pressures.

Social pressure is important, though, and even if Emily is not forced by law to give up the records, public pressure may convince her to do so. In these cases, it is important for libraries to have local policy (as suggested in the prior section) to guide them through the challenge. These policies can look very different (providing different levels of privacy/confidentiality assurances to patrons) from one library to the next. Some libraries state that they will provide redacted patron records (so it would be possible to see, for instance, what books the library has loaned, but not who loaned them), such as Wichita (KS) public library.[16] Powers Memorial Library in Wisconsin provides a definition of terms within its policy, which is important for patrons to understand the responsibilities of the library and their rights in regard to privacy and confidentiality and to receive information about patron records.[17] The library's policy also states that item transaction records will be deleted 90 days after an item is returned to the library. Other libraries, like New York University Libraries, simply reiterate the library's adherence to state law.[18]

WHAT DOES THE ALA SAY?

As noted by Scott Seaman, the first "official" affirmation of the patron privacy was in the 1938 edition of the American Library Association's Code of Ethics for Librarians (technically adopted in 1939 at the Midwinter meeting).[19] The code states that all information acquired from patrons must be treated as confidential by the librarian. You may read this Code of Ethics for yourself: http://www.ala.org/tools/ethics.

The American Library Association has a policy on confidentiality of library records that was first passed in 1971 and most recently amended in 1986. The policy states:

The Council of the American Library Association strongly recommends that the responsible officers of each library, cooperative system, and consortium in the United States:

1. Formally adopt a policy that specifically recognizes its circulation records and other records identifying the names of library users to be confidential.

2. Advise all librarians and library employees that such records shall not be made available to any agency of state, federal, or local government except pursuant to such process, order or subpoena as may be authorized under the authority of, and pursuant to, federal, state, or local law relating to civil, criminal, or administrative discovery procedures or legislative investigative power.
3. Resist the issuance of enforcement of any such process, order, or subpoena until such time as a proper showing of good cause has been made in a court of competent jurisdiction.[20]

This policy also appeals to the Core Values of Librarianship, as privacy is one of these core values.

In addition, ALA provides a detailed guide for responding to law enforcement requests for library patron information.[21] If—and only if—a law enforcement official is able to present a signed warrant to collect patron records, based on probable cause that a crime has occurred and that the patron records are crucial to identifying the culprit, then the library must provide this information. A hunch is not a warrant. A law enforcement official cannot say accessing the records may help them identify offenders, without substantial evidence to support this claim, and simply gain access to any records they want. In Emily's case, the officer has no legal right to access the records without the library's permission. The issue Emily and her staff are more likely to face is whether social pressure from the public or the officers causes them to cave.

In such a case where public pressure mounts, library employees may feel isolated or without support to hold to the position they know, legally and ethically, is correct. The American Library Association can provide some assistance if this case arises. While the ALA's Office for Intellectual Freedom primarily offers support for book challenges, guidance in the case of a challenge to confidentiality policy can also fall under its purview.

WHAT DO OTHER FIELDS SAY?

In this case, other fields can really be a mixed bag of advice. In the field of computer science, there are those who are adamant defenders of privacy as well as those who see users' records as just another way to increase profits. As will be discussed in later chapters, Internet features like cookies (data about the sites you visit) can be used to create direct advertising and monitor user behavior. Internet service providers and web advertisers generally see a lot of positive potential for this collection. Other professions hold patient records very confidentially. They have gone so far as to ensure privacy of data. In the field of medicine, legislation was passed (Health Insurance Portability and Accountability Act, or HIPAA) that mandates the privacy of patient records; however, there are stipulations (not dissimilar from those some might wish to see for libraries) that if patient information can reduce the likelihood of an imminent threat to personal or public safety, then it may be disclosed to law enforcement.

Government records are subject to a variety of rules based on the specific nature of the record. Motor vehicle information like your name, birth date, and license number is available to the public, and other information like your address may be released to certain entities (like motor vehicle insurers).[22] Court records, other than those where a minor is a party, are publicly available. Welfare and tax information, on the other hand, are generally held strictly confidential unless permission is given to disclose this information to specific agencies (such as financial aid services). Specific legislation pertaining to government records varies based on data type and jurisdiction (very similar to current library confidentiality policy).[23]

In academia, protocols like Institutional Review Board (IRB) approval of research activities often have specific measures to ensure privacy and confidentiality. Generally, IRB measures include that confidentiality should be maintained if sharing the information could cause harm to the participants (often "harm" is defined very broadly, essentially meaning that a researcher should always maintain confidentiality). However, the nature of the research is more important than the IRB procedures in determining whether researchers can be compelled by law enforcement agencies to breach confidentiality. For instance, medical researchers can obtain a Certificate of Confidentiality from the National Institutes of Health. This certificate ensures that the researchers cannot be compelled to provide information about participants to law enforcement, or in court.[24] Outside of the Certificate of Confidentiality, whether confidentiality can actually be assured to research participants is a murky issue. Certainly, a good researcher will defend the confidentiality of the information, but could still be legally compelled to share it.

Common among these fields is that the majority of professionals want to protect the privacy and confidentiality of those they serve, but also that there are forces (online retailers, law enforcement, members of the public) that they must fight against to ensure those rights. Libraries are by no means alone in the fight to ensure the confidentiality of the information of those they serve. They can find allies in virtually every field.

WHAT DO RESEARCHERS SAY?

Several researchers rightly note that the USA PATRIOT Act was a "game changer" for patron privacy.[25] The law allowed certain government officials, with an official court order, the right to search a library and its records.[26] Library researchers at the time were clearly concerned about how the legislation may be used to justify widespread spying on the reading habits of library patrons. In *Libraries, Policy, and Politics in a Democracy*, Paul Jaeger and colleagues name the PATRIOT Act as the start of the historical epoch known as the *Intervention Years*, a period of increased control over libraries by government through legislation and funding control.[27] Before the PATRIOT Act became law, information requests were more likely to come from patrons, such as parents inquiring about their child's checkout history. It is one thing to work with a parent that is angry but a completely different thing to work with a government that is angry, especially in a public library where the government plays a role in funding.

In response to what Jaeger et al. term the Intervention Years, there have been calls (especially among Jaeger and colleagues) to not only develop library policy but also to become politically active and engaged as a library ("political" in this case meaning library-advocate, not Democrat or Republican).[28] Many of the state laws related to confidentiality of patron records date back three decades or more. Libraries (and state library organizations) can become advocates for updating these laws and, to the greatest extent possible, mitigating the invasion of confidentiality permitted by the PATRIOT Act and related legislation. Libraries may also be more proactive in educating the public about why insuring information privacy is important, developing a more informed electorate.

Seaman notes that some might argue that public library patron records may be considered government information and thus subject to open records laws.[29] This was why it was so important for states to pass laws specifically protecting patron records (as with the earlier examples of Kansas and California). Similarly, libraries should have policies in place guiding the restriction of access to patron records; in the absence of such policies, it could be argued that the library is willing to waive its right to enforce patron privacy law. Magi suggests that, as of 2007, fewer than one-half of the libraries in her home state of Vermont had a patron confidentiality policy in place.[30] Magi also notes, however, that the issue is not that library directors/stakeholders do not believe patron confidentiality is important, but rather that they simply have not *gotten around* to codifying privacy practices in a written policy. Again, this could lead to serious problems if and when an individual/entity attempts to compel library employees to share patron record information.

For libraries that do not currently have a privacy/confidentiality policy in place, there are several case studies and checklists published in the professional literature and by professional organizations that provide insight on how the process of developing such a policy transpired. Hess, LaPorte-Fiori, and Engwall published a description of their experience at Oakland (MI) University.[31] The Illinois Library Association has published a checklist of best practices for developing patron confidentiality policy, authored by Trina

Magi, which can be found on its website.[32] Of course, the ALA is also a tremendous source of information on the development of privacy/confidentiality policy: http://www.ala.org/advocacy/privacy/toolkit/policy. These cases and checklists demonstrate that the development of a policy from scratch is a major task, but one that is not impossible.

WHAT DO WE SAY?

This crisis is one where we feel very confident in our perspective as to what should be done. First, research the library patron privacy policies applicable to your patrons. It is possible this information will be provided by your state library; however, it is also readily available from the American Library Association at this link: http://www.ala.org/advocacy/privacy/statelaws. Based on what is outlined in state law, craft patron privacy guidelines that state the rights of patrons to confidentiality of records. Generally, the policy, across all libraries, should state that library records will not be turned over to law enforcement officials unless a signed warrant is supplied. Depending on the library's situation, it may also be stipulated that an attorney representing the library will review the warrant before any records are turned over to the officials (this would be ideal if feasible, as it will help ensure that the warrant meets the government standards to be valid and that only records named in the warrant are requisitioned).[33] If it is possible to communicate with library/city attorneys and officials during this process, it may prove immensely beneficial to ensure the policy is "airtight."

One example of an excellent confidentiality policy is that of the University of Illinois at Urbana-Champaign. This policy page begins by providing a list of policies and legal documents that compel/inform the policy, including the American Library Association's policy manual, the Family Education Rights and Privacy Act, and the State of Illinois's library confidentiality act.[34] The actual policy is then listed, followed by specific examples of cases in which patron information will explicitly not be shared. We believe this is a good example of a confidentiality policy, as it provides justification for the policy (shielding the library from claims that the policy is arbitrary or without basis) and provides specific examples of how the policy will be enforced, which informs both library employees and patrons on how the library will respond to a request before the request is made.

Second, prepare library employees to react appropriately when a request for patrons' records is made. Preparation will help those employees feel less intimidated should someone *important* come along and ask for records. Make sure the policy is enforced consistently. This means that if you do not let the police have access to a teen's records, then a parent probably should not have access either (while law enforcement officers are the example used throughout this chapter, they are by no means the only party that would like to bend library policy to get their hands on patron records).

Finally, communication is key. Once a policy is in place, share it with stakeholders, especially patrons. Let those who use your library know that their privacy is of utmost concern for the library and that everything possible will be done to keep records confidential. This will help put patrons at ease (while also making them more alert about privacy concerns in their information use behavior).

These are fairly basic, intuitive steps, but steps that are nonetheless vitally important and often neglected by libraries. By creating policy now, rather than waiting until an incident prompts it, libraries can prevent a major headache (or worse). We hope that by seeing what others have done in regard to preserving patron privacy, you will be better prepared to develop policies that leave patrons feeling rightly confident in their privacy while using your library's resources.

CONCLUSION

In this chapter, we discussed the importance of policy—at both the state and individual library levels—in preserving the confidentiality of patron records. All libraries should have a policy in place to protect themselves from records requests that are not accompanied by a legal warrant for the seizure of property. Policy, and consistent enforcement, is important for ensuring that patrons feel at greater ease in using library resources.

While the solution—at least among libraries in the United States—is by and large the same for all libraries, that does not make it an easy one. One can easily see the benefit in sharing information that might identify or help convict a criminal. However, a fundamental aspect of librarians' work is guaranteeing that all patrons have access and feel comfort in acquiring the information they need. This is impossible when patrons lack trust in the library. Only strict adherence to a confidentiality policy can give all patrons comfort in seeking and finding information within the library's walls.

NOTES

1. Trina J. Magi, "The gap between theory and practice: A study of the prevalence and strength of patron confidentiality policies in public and academic libraries," *Library and Information Science Research* 29, no. 4 (2007): 455–470.

2. James B. Comey, "Fighting terrorism and preserving civil liberties," *University of Richmond Law Review* 40 (2005): 405–407.

3. Heather MacNeil, *Without consent: The ethics of disclosing personal information in public archives* (Chicago, IL: Society of American Archivists, 1992); Mayo Taylor and William Black, "In search of reason: Libraries and the USA PATRIOT Act," *Journal of Librarianship and Information Science* 36, no. 2 (2004): 51–54.

4. Sandra Hirsh and Susan Alman, *Blockchain (Library Futures Series, Book 3)* (Chicago, IL: ALA Neal-Schuman, 2019); Carrie Smith, "Blockchain reaction: How library professionals are approaching blockchain technology and its potential impact," *American Libraries*, retrieved March 1, 2019. https://americanlibrariesmagazine.org/2019/03/01/library-blockchain-reaction/

5. Melanie Swan, *Blockchain: Blueprint for a new economy* (Sebastopol, CA: O'Reilly, 2015).

6. Ralph Merkle, "Protocols for public key cryptosystems," *Proceedings of the 1980 Symposium on Security and Privacy* (1980): 122–133.

7. Deepak Puthal, Nisha Malik, Saraju Mohanty, Elias Kougianos, and Chi Yang, "The blockchain as a decentralized security framework," *IEEE* (2018). https://www.researchgate.net/profile/Saraju_Mohanty/publication/323491592_The_Blockchain_as_a_Decentralized_Security_Framework_Future_Directions/links/5aa202e5aca272d448b4c297/The-Blockchain-as-a-Decentralized-Security-Framework-Future-Directions.pdf

8. Stefan Brands, *Rethinking public key infrastructures and digital certificates* (Cambridge, MA: MIT Press, 2000).

9. Stacey L. Bowers, "Privacy and library records," *Journal of Academic Librarianship* 32, no. 4 (2006): 377–383.

10. American Libraries, *Connecticut four reunite against FBI overreach*, retrieved July 2, 2019. https://americanlibrariesmagazine.org/blogs/the-scoop/connecticut-four-librarians-fbi-overreach

11. South Central Library System, *Before the police arrive*, retrieved July 7, 2019. https://www.scls.info/management/law/enforcement/police

12. Cornell University Library, *Library procedure for handling requests for patron information*, retrieved July 7, 2019. https://www.library.cornell.edu/about/policies/requests-for-patron-information

13. Jean Preer, *Library ethics* (Westport, CT: Libraries Unlimited, 2008): 186.

14. State of Kansas, Kansas statutes chapter 45: Public records, documents and information, retrieved May 23, 2019. https://www.ksrevisor.org/statutes/ksa_ch45.html

15. State of California, *California government code 6267: Registration and circulation records of library supported by public funds*, retrieved May 26, 2019. https://codes.findlaw.com/ca/government-code/gov-sect-6267.html

16. Wichita Public Library, *Privacy policy*, retrieved July 27, 2019. http://www.wichitalibrary.org/confidentiality-of-library-records

17. Powers Memorial Library, *Policy on confidentiality of library records*, retrieved July 3, 2019. http://www.palmyra.lib.wi.us/policy-on-confidentiality -of-library-records

18. New York University Libraries, *Library records confidentiality policy*, retrieved October 2, 2019. http://library.nyu.edu/about/visiting/policies/library -records-confidentiality-policy

19. Scott Seaman, "Confidentiality of patron records in electronic library circulation systems," *18th Regional Conference on the History and Philosophy of Science* (1994). https://files.eric.ed.gov/fulltext/ED371723.pdf

20. American Library Association Council, *Policy on confidentiality of library records*, retrieved October 18, 2019. http://www.ala.org/advocacy/intfreedom /statementspols/otherpolicies/policyconfidentiality

21. American Library Association, *Suggested guidelines: How to respond to law enforcement requests for library records and user information*, retrieved August 7, 2019. http://www.ala.org/advocacy/privacy/lawenforcement/guidelines

22. Privacy Rights Clearinghouse, *Government records and your privacy*, retrieved September 19, 2019. https://www.privacyrights.org/consumer-guides /government-records-and-your-privacy

23. International Comparative Legal Guides, *USA data protection laws and regulations 2020*, retrieved May 8, 2019. https://iclg.com/practice-areas/data -protection-laws-and-regulations/usa

24. Devon K. Check, Leslie E. Wolf, Lauren A. Dame, and Laura M. Beskow, "Certificates of confidentiality and informed consent: Perspectives of IRB chairs and institutional legal counsel," *IRB: Ethics and Human Research* 36, no. 1 (2014): 1–8.

25. Kathryn Martin, "The USA PATRIOT Act's application to library patron records," *Journal of Legislation* 29 (2003): 283–306; Paul T. Jaeger, Ursula Gorham, Lindsay Sarin and John C. Bertot, "Libraries, policy, and politics in a democracy: Four historical epochs," *Library Quarterly* 83, no. 2 (2014): 166–181; Mayo Taylor and William Black, "In search of reason: Libraries and the USA PATRIOT Act," *Journal of Librarianship and Information Science* 36, no. 2 (2004): 51–54.

26. Kathryn Martin, "The USA PATRIOT Act's application to library patron records," *Journal of Legislation* 29 (2003): 283–306.

27. Jaeger et al., "Libraries, policy, and politics."

28. Paul T. Jaeger and Lindsay C. Sarin, "The politically engaged public library: Admitting and embracing the political nature of libraries and their goals," *Public Library Quarterly* 35, no. 4 (2016): 325–330.

29. Seaman, "Confidentiality of patron records."

30. Magi, "The gap between theory and practice."

31. Amanda Nichols Hess, Rachelle LaPorte-Fiori, and Keith Engwall, "Preserving patron privacy in the 21st century academic library," *Journal of Academic Librarianship* 41, no. 1 (2015): 105–114.

32. Trina J. Magi, *Protecting library patron confidentiality: Checklist of best practices,* retrieved July 23, 2019. https://www.ila.org/advocacy/making-your -case/privacy/confidentiality-best-practices

33. Wichita Public Library, *Privacy policy,* retrieved July 26, 2019. http:// www.wichitalibrary.org/confidentiality-of-library-records

34. University of Illinois at Urbana-Champaign, *Confidentiality policy,* retrieved August 6, 2019. https://www.library.illinois.edu/geninfo/policies /confidential

THREE

Photography and Video Recording within the Library and Social Media Policy

Kathy is a library security officer at the Library of Make Believe, a large, metropolitan library in the northeastern United States. One of her primary duties is to diffuse conflicts between patrons that occur on library property. One day, an argument breaks out between two patrons in an adult reading area. As Kathy makes her way over to the area, one of the patrons (we will call her Kim) explains that someone stole her water bottle and accuses the other patron (Janice) of being the thief. Janice, in response, begins to shout expletives at Kim.

Kim pulls out her phone and begins to record a video of Janice's actions. After Kathy arrives, both Kim and Janice appear to settle down, though neither is particularly happy with the other. Though Janice consents to a search of her backpack that reveals that she does not have the water bottle, Kim still believes she is the thief. Janice begins to worry that the video Kim recorded will end up on social media and demands that she delete it. Kim refuses. Janice then turns to Kathy and demands that the library confiscate the phone and delete the video.

Kathy considers several ethical quandaries: Does library policy allow for the video to be recorded on library property? What is the procedure to follow now that the video has been recorded? Is the library or the accused allowed to stop the video from being posted online?

Kathy realizes that her library has no policy in place to answer any of these questions. Instead of being able to handle the problem in-house, she *has to call the local cops, which draws attention to the scene and disrupts the activities of other patrons in the library.*

TAPING THE POLICE AND DRAG QUEEN STORY TIME

Probably the most controversial version of this story is whether it is legal to record police officers on cell phones during traffic stops and arrests. According to an excellent infographic from the American Civil Liberties Union of Connecticut, you have the right to record in any public, outdoor space any activity, including that of police officers, though, as Dina Mishra noted in 2007, audio recording laws can vary widely from state to state.[1] Indoors and on private property, individuals may only take images/record video if it is allowed by the property owner—even images/recordings of the police—and recording without permission may result in expulsion from the property as well as trespassing charges.

If a police officer is performing their duty in a public space (like a city street) or private property where you are the property owner, then photography/recording (though perhaps not audio recording) is perfectly legal and cannot be impeded. Inside the library, however, the rules are up to the property owner/administrator (the library administration), so libraries have the legal right to force individuals taking photographs/recording to either stop doing so or face trespassing charges. Yet it is important for libraries to have consistent policy in place to guide how they will enforce their right to allow or prevent photography and video recording.

Another case where photography in the library has been highly controversial is with news reporting of book challenges and drag queen story time events. These are cases where people want access (whether it be to photograph some "evidence" of a malfeasance on the part of the library or to capitalize on the discussion by publishing news stories), and libraries may be inclined not to provide it, because if the challenge or event is too sensationalized, it could result in unfair public perception or even violence toward the library or event participants. The people who want access *will* scrutinize the library's photography and videography policy, and there are plenty of instances of outrage because a library did not have a policy that restricted photography/videography but decided to ban it anyway (which, again, is fully within their rights, but looks bad in the public eye).[2] Waiting until an incident occurs to put a policy in place just adds fodder for those who want to go after libraries (Dan Kleinman, anyone?).[3]

Of course, the modern concern is not only that photographs/video will be taken but how broadly and quickly they will be shared. Social media makes sharing an image to viewers around the globe as simple as tapping a screen. Yet many libraries still lack a social media sharing policy. Libraries have the power to limit both the capturing of images and video and the sharing of this content, but they give away that power when they put no policy in place.

WHAT DO PRACTICING LIBRARIANS SAY?

Generally, practicing librarians who have spoken on this issue tend to mirror the perspective of their libraries. This does not seem to be a controversial issue so much as it is an issue about which very few are thinking. Among the Twitter, Instagram, and listserv worlds, we could not find this topic discussed at any point in the last half decade. There are a few Twitter comments from patrons requesting information about photography policy from their libraries, but again these are limited to a few posts over a half-decade period. So we will dive right into library policy.

WHAT DOES LIBRARY POLICY SAY?

Library policy pertaining to photography varies widely. Stanford University Libraries prohibits photography within all library building, except when prior permission is obtained.[4] Saint Paul (MN) Public Library also requires individuals to received advance approval before taking any pictures or video.[5] Wichita (KS) Public Library allows for noncommercial photography of specific library spaces (lobby, study, and program areas), but restricts photography in other areas (stacks, archival materials) and bars most photography of people within the library.[6] At the (Washington) DC Public Library, amateur (no tripods or lighting) photography is permitted in all public areas (not including stacks and private meeting/study rooms).[7] Boulder (CO) Public Library permits photography and video recording by visitors, but also reserves the right to stop any photography that might compromise "public safety or security," which could be interpreted broadly in the case of photography during a conflict.[8]

The University of Illinois has published a decision tree for photographers to determine whether permission is needed (Figure 3.1).[9] This tree is one of few library policies to address images of individuals, requiring that verbal assent be received from any identifiable individuals before any images are taken. MIT Libraries requires consent of parents for all noncommercial photography of minors and photo release forms for all commercial photography.[10]

At the Library of Congress, photography is a complex matter. This is due to its status as a research library, museum (of sorts), event center, and federal

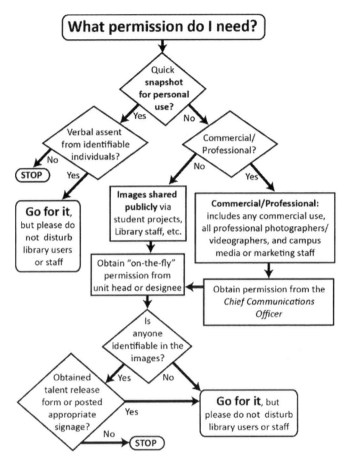

Figure 3.1   Decision Tree for Photography in University Library, University of Illinois Urbana-Champaign
Reprinted with permission.

building. For security purposes, photography/videography of library exteriors technically requires prior permission. Photography within the visitor spaces of the library is permitted, but no special equipment is allowed. Group photography (more than five people) is prohibited. Photography is not permitted at the reading room overlook (though that did not stop at least one of us on our last trip . . .). There are many other photography-restricted areas throughout the premises.

The only consistent thing about library photography policy is its inconsistency. Libraries can range from having no policy at all to having a decision tree like the University of Illinois. Photography/videography policy does not seem like a complex topic. It is simply a topic that is being overlooked, resulting in no unity in policy.

WHAT DOES THE ALA SAY?

The American Library Association provides surprisingly little guidance in this area. Perhaps the closest to any direct answer is the section on "social networking tools" in the *Developing or Revising a Library Privacy Policy* document.[11] This is the only direct mention of video recording by patrons in a library published on the ALA website. The ALA policy tied to this guide, however, simply indicates the importance of allowing patrons to participate in social media activities in the library, which provides little help to Kathy's scenario.

We may be able to infer from other privacy topics discussed in ALA publications the organization's likely belief on the matter of photography and video recording. Generally, the organization comes down on the side of both patrons' rights and patrons' privacy.[12] Based on this, we might assume that photography/videography would be permitted within the library except when it infringes on the privacy of other patrons. In the case of the disruptive patron experienced by Kathy, it is likely that asking both patrons involved in the dispute to leave the property or face trespassing charges would be advised. There is no evidence in ALA documentation that they would recommend confiscating patron property for any reason other than an immediate threat to the safety of the library or other patrons (and this would have to be loosely interpreted to justify the inclusion of photography/video recording as an "immediate threat").

The American Library Association does provide a direct (though, we might say, incomplete) response on the topic of library employees taking photos of patrons. In an ALA Q&A blog post, a user asks "if ALA has a policy in relation to taking pictures of children or adults in the library and then using them for promotional purposes."[13] The response posted by ALA is that no such policy exists. The organization does, however, encourage the use of photo release forms any time a photo is taken where a patron is identifiable.

WHAT DO OTHER FIELDS SAY?

As demonstrated in the prior two chapters, there are a great many similarities noted in this section between librarianship and the medical professions. These are likely two of the professions that hold information privacy most sacred. That is no different for the problem of photography and recording. There is extensive literature in medical sciences that discusses the ethics of photography of physicians/surgeons/nurses, patients, and medical center visitors. Because the Health Insurance Portability and Accountability Act (HIPAA) requires patient information to be confidential, many researchers argue this law applies to photography of patients when they enter a health facility.[14] HIPAA does not apply to one patient sharing information with another patient, however, so while it might provide direction in regard to medical professionals and assistants taking pictures of patients, it does not necessarily provide direction in regard to other patients doing so.

Generally, schools ban photography within their premises unless granted rights to do so by the administration.[15] The rationale for this is fairly straightforward. For privacy reasons, no person should have a photograph taken of them without their permission (this holds true for many library photography policies, as we have discussed); the "persons" in this case are also minors, which makes them especially vulnerable—not only would the student's permission be needed for a photograph, but the caretaker's permission as well. If your library has a large number of patrons who are minors, having some policy that specifically addresses photography of minors would likely be a helpful reminder that caretaker permission is required in addition to the permission of the minor.

Photography in museums tends to be a little more lenient than many libraries toward non-commercial photography and much stricter toward commercial photography. The Smithsonian museums permit noncommercial photography in all public spaces, as do the Chicago Institute of Art and Field Musuem.[16] Generally, the only museums that seem to significantly limit photography are those where the item(s) on display are vulnerable to deterioration (e.g., old manuscripts and photographs).

Stephanie Johnson conducted excellent master's thesis research on the topic of museum photography policy in 2014. As we have found in our search for library photography policy research, Johnson found that no literature exists on establishing a museum photography policy.[17] Johnson classified museum photography policies into three categories—open photo, prohibitive photo, and photo with exceptions. Seventy-six percent of museums she surveyed had what she classified as photo with exceptions policy (e.g., fragile object, traveling exhibitions, intellectual property rights). Five percent had an open photo policy (no restrictions), while the remaining 19 percent had prohibitive (strict) photo policy.[18] She also found (as did our findings among libraries) that policies could vary widely in length and content. Her final recommendation to museum professionals: "visitor photography policy itself should be clear and transparent."[19]

Each private organization is able to set its own policy in regard to photography.[20] For many organizations, particularly those that sell goods directly to consumers (e.g., Walmart, Old Navy), that policy is "no photography allowed." Of course, in these cases, it is often a matter of making it more difficult to browse goods in a physical store, take photos of goods they want to purchase, and then search for cheaper prices online. Nonetheless, many of these organizations also want to avoid any backlash that might come their way as a result of permitting photography/videography of other consumers.

WHAT DO RESEARCHERS SAY?

Though the main focus is only tangentially related to the topic of this chapter, Cotter and Sasso's 2016 article "Libraries Protecting Privacy on Social Media" provides valuable insight into library administrators/employees' perspectives on privacy and photography in the library.[21] Their survey received 257 respondents across all library types. One concerning finding is that the majority of library social media policies are developed by one or a small group of library employees, as opposed to a library board or collective of all library employees and/or stakeholders. This makes it unlikely that these policies are being vetted, and they may not even be in the best interest of the library as a whole. There was also significant disagreement among respondents as to whether sharing photos of patrons on social media without their permission compromises patron privacy. This suggests some disagreement over what conditions a library's photography policy should contain; permission may not be as important to some librarians/libraries as other sources of information (discussed in this chapter) suggest it should be.

Bryan Carson developed guidelines for photography in libraries based on his research of privacy law and library service and, subsequently, published a related article on the topic of social media.[22] Carson reiterates what is stated earlier in this chapter in regard to the need to have a written consent form and to have caretaker permission for minors. He also lists what elements should be included in this consent form: to whom consent is being given (whether it is the library for marketing, or an individual or organization coming from outside of the library), for which pictures is consent being given, for what purpose will the pictures be used, a release of rights (essentially a statement that you have permission to re-/produce the picture and the subject will not sue you), an acknowledgment that the signee is over age 18 and understands the consent they are providing, and a location for signature and date.[23]

WHAT DO WE SAY?

We like the idea used by the University of Illinois to create a decision tree for photographers so much so that we created our own for the Library of Make Believe (Figure 3.2). We recommend this as an excellent way to convey information about library policy. The tree can be as simple or complex as needed

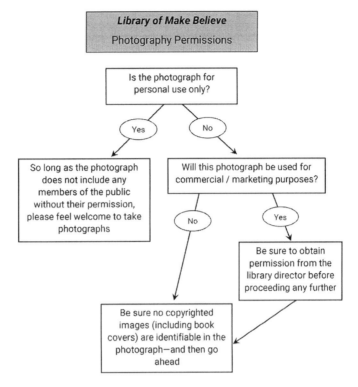

Figure 3.2   Decision Tree for Photography in the Library of Make Believe

for your library. It is also important to stipulate what happens if the policy is broken, such as temporary confiscation of the device, deletion of (or copyright suit against) any recording, or contact with the police.

When confronted with the situation of the patron making the video recording, Kathy will now be able to negotiate it like a pro. The policy tree clearly indicates that permission must be obtained for any recording of another patron, thus the recording made by the angry patron is in violation of library policy. She must then follow library policy to confiscate the device and ask the patron to wait in a back office until the police arrive and determine what should be done with the recording.

By the end of this book, we may just have to rename it *Everything We Do Wrong and University of Illinois Library Does Right*. This is the second chapter where we have really identified U of I's policy as the best around. This is not due to any bias on our part, but just speaks to the clearly great detail put forth by this organization to ensure that no question is left unanswered or puts the university at risk. If you want a companion to this book (or just want to know how to do most everything right in general), check out U of I Library's website: https://www.library.illinois.edu/.

SOCIAL MEDIA USE POLICY IN LIBRARIES

In this special section of the book (special in the sense that we recognized, after planning out the book, that we needed to go back and include this or the chapter would feel incomplete), we will provide an overview of social media policy in libraries. Social media policy is often related to photography policy, in that the biggest complaints about social media in libraries is that it is intrusive (e.g., people taking pictures of spaces/people and sharing it on Twitter or Instagram) or offensive (inappropriate posts by patrons on library pages). This section has the same structure as the full chapters but is condensed, without the headings.

According to a survey distributed by WebJunction in late 2017, nearly 40 percent of library respondents claimed their libraries had no social media policy (the sampling for survey was biased, because it was distributed to participants in a webinar called "Libraries and Social Media," but nonetheless indicates that many libraries did not have a policy).[24] Though virtually all libraries are using social media, a large number are doing nothing to police its use by staff and patrons either online or on the library premises.[25] In the absence of a policy (and even with it), libraries can find themselves butting heads with a frequent ally, the First Amendment of the U.S. Constitution.

Many libraries have extensive policies for interacting on social media, but limited policy on using/sharing on social media within the library. This is the case with the Cook Memorial Public Library District (IL), which has a policy that includes six articles detailing all aspects of participating on library social media, from library-sponsored content rules to what content shared by patrons is and is not appropriate.[26] Jackson County libraries (MN) combine a social media and photography policy, stating that photographs taken during library events may be shared on social media.[27]

The ALA actually provides very clear guidance as to social media policy for posting and interaction (though less clear guidance on use of social media on devices within the library).[28] The guidelines suggest that library policy should clearly define acceptable behavior and the consequences if users engage in unacceptable behavior. Generally, this can be difficult to define and defend, as users can claim their First Amendment right to free speech; however, there is unprotected speech that can be removed with fairly strong certainty that no legitimate concern will arise: "copyright violations, obscenity, child pornography, defamatory or libelous comments, or imminent or true threats against the library, library staff, or other users."[29] Libraries should clearly state that such posts will be removed and what, if any, will be the consequences for the user (e.g., banning from the page).

ALA's report also states that all libraries should include a disclaimer on their social media pages that comments expressed on the pages do not necessarily reflect those of the library or its employees.[30] Also included could be a statement of privacy (any information shared on the page will not be collected or used by the library in any way), contact information for the page administrators, and information for users who have a complaint or challenge to their removal from the page or the library in general. Including this information reduces the liability on the library for content shared on the page. In addition to including this information directly on the social media pages, it may also be shared on a library web page or alongside the other privacy policies.

Some researchers have suggested that social media policy be informed by the sensibilities of the users. For instance, Anuja Jain and colleagues suggest that student ratings of appropriateness for social media postings could be used to inform policy and practice at a university medical center.[31] This type of user-centered design does seemingly appeal to the values of librarianship, but the product may not necessarily be in the best interest of the library.

The American Association of Museums published a social media handbook in 2011. This handbook introduces various social media platforms and provides a sample social media policy. In this sample policy, it is recommended that institutions list all social media platforms in which they participate (on their website), provide guidelines as to what content is inappropriate for sharing on the sites, and state that any content shared on the pages is public and thus discretion is advised.[32]

Library social media policies have been researched and written about in several scholarly publications. Louise Cadell pondered, in a 2013 article, whether it is even appropriate to have a social media policy in a cultural history institution, as such policies seemingly contradict the purpose of social media and of these institutions. Cadell studied institutions in Queensland, Australia, conducting interviews with their employees. She concluded that "it is practical for cultural heritage institutions to have a social media policy if it inspires confidence, empowers practitioners, and encourages them to use social media."[33]

Peacemaker, Robinson, and Hurst take a public relations approach to developing social media policy.[34] Their article walks through the concerns that they had when developing a policy, the background research they conducted, their receptivity to change, and their system for publishing the policy. Their policy was informed by a survey of academic librarians from across the United States, which indicated that clear content strategies and constant evaluation are important aspects of creating and maintaining a social media platform.

Elizabeth Breed discussed the process of developing a social media policy at Capital Area District Library (MI) in a 2013 article.[35] Breed explains the process of continuously updating social media policy to reflect evolving technology and changes within the library's organizational structure. She also describes how important the examples of others were to the development and updates of the policy (perhaps this book would have been helpful back then). Policy is a living document that must be treated as such when new technologies and ideas challenge the paradigm from which it was originally formed.

We would recommend that all libraries have a social media policy that stipulates what content is appropriate to share and reduces liability by stating that opinions shared on the library's social media do not necessarily reflect those of the library. One would probably be well advised to integrate a photography policy into the social media policy, since most photos that will be taken within the library will ultimately be shared on a social media platform. Having a policy that guides whether patrons need permission to take images for sharing on Instagram or other social platforms may be necessary. This is different from images taken only for personal use; the images are being shared publicly.

CONCLUSION

Virtually all libraries have a policy in regard to photography and videography. These policies, however, can vary widely in terms of detail. Recent incidents involving confrontation between patrons in the library and events like drag queen story time demonstrate the importance of having a specific, detailed policy in place. Many libraries, especially the University of Illinois, provide a strong model for how such a policy can be crafted. Libraries should work with stakeholders to craft the most appropriate policy for their specific population.

Libraries should also consider whether it is beneficial to have a social media policy in place. In the case that social media becomes disruptive (e.g., taking Instagram pictures in front of the circulation desk), a policy may prove helpful; however, it is important not to alienate patrons by being restrictive toward such a ubiquitous communication channel. At minimum, having a policy to guide user behaviors when interacting with the library's social media pages online will likely prove beneficial if any violation/inappropriate conduct occurs. The need to have a policy, and the extent of the policy, may vary from library to library.

In the first part of this book, we have learned about the importance of having privacy policy in place within all libraries. It provides an important buffer between the library and those who may oppose the right to privacy. In the following chapters of part two, we will investigate what libraries can do when faced with challenges to their policies.

NOTES

1. America Civil Liberties Union of Connecticut, *Know your rights: Recording the police*, retrieved July 28, 2019. https://www.acluct.org/sites/default/files/field_documents/know_your_rights-_recording_the_police_11.pdf; Dina Mishra, "Undermining excessive privacy for police: Citizen tape recording to check police officers' power," *Yale Law Journal* 117, no. 7 (2007): 1549–1570.

2. Elizabeth LaFleur, *Hundreds hold competing protests at Drag Queen Story Hour as deputies block media entry*, retrieved February 17, 2019. https://www.greenvilleonline.com/story/news/2019/02/17/drag-queen-story-hour-draws-crowds-competing-protests/2899862002/; Dan Kleinman, *FOIA request of Houston Public Library by SafeLibraries*, retrieved March 23, 2019. https://safelibraries.blogspot.com/2019/03/foia-request-3-houston-public-library.html

3. Katie Frankowicz, *Astoria Library updates user conduct policy*, retrieved April 16, 2019. https://www.dailyastorian.com/news/local/astoria-library-updates-user-conduct-policy/article_0ce52d6e-6054-11e9-8550-7b53af93dc64.html

4. Stanford University Libraries, *Photography in library buildings*, retrieved July 19, 2019. https://library.stanford.edu/using/special-policies/photography-library-buildings

5. Saint Paul Public Library, *Photography and videography*, retrieved July 19, 2019. https://sppl.org/policies/photography-and-videography

6. Wichita Public Library, *Policies*, retrieved September 29, 2019. http://www.wichitalibrary.org/About/Policies/Pages/filming-photography.aspx

7. DC Public Library, *Policy on photography at the DC Public Library*, retrieved November 18, 2019. https://www.dclibrary.org/node/3161

8. Boulder Public Library, *Photography and video recording policy*, retrieved November 19, 2019. https://boulderlibrary.org/about/rules/photography-and-video-recording-policy/

9. University of Illinois University Library, *Photographic, video, and audio recording inside library facilities*, retrieved October 21, 2019. https://www.library.illinois.edu/geninfo/policies/recording_guidelines/

10. Massachusetts Institute of Technology Libraries, *Photo policy*, retrieved August 21, 2019. https://libraries.mit.edu/about/policies/photo-policy/

11. American Library Association, *Developing or revising a library privacy policy*, retrieved December 2, 2019. http://www.ala.org/advocacy/privacy/toolkit/policy

12. American Library Association, *Privacy: An interpretation of the library bill of rights*, retrieved June 24, 2019. http://www.ala.org/advocacy/intfreedom/librarybill/interpretations/privacy

13. American Library Association, *Libraries and photos of patrons*, retrieved August 11, 2019. http://www.ala.org/tools/libraries-and-photos-patrons

14. Avinash Supe, "Ethical considerations in medical photography," *Issues in Medical Ethics* 11, no. 3 (2003): 83–84.

15. Kent County Council, *The use of cameras and images within educational settings*, retrieved October 21, 2019. https://www.kelsi.org.uk/__data/assets/pdf_file/0008/28484/Policy-and-Guidance-for-Kent-Schools-About-Photography-in-Schools.pdf

16. Smithsonian Institution, *Visitor tips*, retrieved June 14, 2019. https://naturalhistory.si.edu/visit/visitor-tips; Art Institute of Chicago, *FAQs*, retrieved July 19, 2019. https://www.artic.edu/visit/frequently-asked-questions; Field Museum, *Frequently asked questions*, retrieved June 19, 2019. https://www.fieldmuseum.org/visit/frequently-asked-questions

17. Stephanie Johnson, *Visitor photography policy: An exploration of current trends and considerations across American museums* (master's thesis). University of Oregon, 2014.

18. Ibid., 20.

19. Ibid., 64.

20. America Civil Liberties Union of Connecticut, *Know your rights*.

21. Kelley Cotter and Maureen Sasso, "Libraries protecting privacy on social media." *Pennsylvania Libraries: Research and Practice* 4, no. 2 (2016): 73–89.

22. Bryan Carson, "Laws for using photos you take at your library," *Marketing Library Services* 22, no. 5 (2008): 1–3. https://www.nyla.org/images/nyla/files/LawsPhotosLibrary.pdf; Bryan Carson, "Libraries and social media," *Information Outlook* 14, no. 7 (2010): 9–12.

23. Carson, "Laws for using photos," 2.

24. WebJunction, *Social media and libraries survey summary*, retrieved February 16, 2019. https://www.webjunction.org/news/webjunction/social-media-libraries-survey.html

25. Brady D. Lund, "Does public libraries' Facebook following correlate with library usage?," *Journal of Web Librarianship* (2019). https://doi.org/10.1080/19322909.2019.1693943

26. Cook Memorial Public Library District, *Social media policy*, retrieved September 18, 2019. https://www.cooklib.org/social-media-policy

27. Jackson County Library, *Social media policy*, retrieved May 19, 2019. https://jclmn.org/about/library-policies/

28. American Library Association, *Social media guidelines for public and academic libraries*, retrieved June 12, 2019. http://www.ala.org/advocacy/intfreedom/socialmediaguidelines

29. Ibid.

30. Ibid.

31. Anuja Jain, Elizabeth Petty, Reda Jaber, Sean Tackett, Joel Purkiss, James Fitzgerald, and Casey White, "What is appropriate to post on social media?

Ratings from students, faculty members and the public." *Medical Education* 48, no. 2 (2014): 157–169.

32. American Association of Museums, *Social media handbook*, retrieved October 12, 2019. https://web.archive.org/web/20170125145705/https://www .imls.gov/assets/1/AssetManager/AAHC_Convening_MAPSocial.pdf

33. Cadell, Louise, "Socially practical or practically unsociable? A study into social media policy experiences in Queensland cultural heritage institutions," *Australian Academic and Research Libraries* 44, no. 1 (2013): 3–13.

34. Bettina Peacemaker, Sue Robinson, and Emily Hurst, "Connecting best practices in public relations to social media strategies for academic libraries." *College and Undergraduate Libraries* 23, no. 1 (2016): 101–108.

35. Elizabeth Breed, "Creating a social media policy: What we did, what we learned." *Marketing Library Services* 27, no. 2 (2013). https://www.infotoday .com/mls/mar13/Breed--Creating-a-Social-Media-Policy.shtml

FOUR

When Escalation Must Result in Calling the Police

Jake is a circulation desk attendant at a suburban public library. During the daytime hours (about 9 a.m., when the library opens, until 3 p.m.), the main users of the library are older adults and preschool-age children, who attend a variety of programs offered by the library. During this time, Jake's job is not too hectic at all (the youth services coordinator Rosie, on the other hand . . .). However, when the high school lets out at 3 p.m., things rapidly begin to change. By 3:30, teenagers outnumber all other patrons three-to-one. Not that there is anything categorically wrong with teenagers. They are just . . . a lot.

One day as Jake is voting in the American Library Association annual election (like all good librarians do), he hears some yelling coming from one of the library's computer areas. When he approaches the computer area, Jake notices that it suddenly gets very quiet. As he peers around a corner, he sees a group of three adults and five teens sitting near each other at the computer desks. In inquiring what the noise was that he had heard, the two groups suddenly come alive, with the adults suggesting that the teens were fighting amongst one another, while the teens argued that one of the adults shoved them from a chair while they were working on a class assignment. Without a clear indication of which story is true, Jake makes the (probably misguided) decision to warn everyone that their conduct is inappropriate and that another disruption of this type may result in their removal from the library premises. He then returns to his desk to submit his election ballot.

No more than five minutes later, Jake is disrupted while helping a patron find a copy of The Brothers Karamazov *by further yelling from the computer area. This time as Jake approaches the area, it is evident that the argument from earlier has escalated into a near brawl. He jumps in between a teen and adult who look primed to throw punches and is simultaneously pushed by both of them, causing him to fall to the floor and watch helplessly as his glasses fly from his head and tumble several feet away, narrowly avoiding the crushing step of an absent-minded patron walking by the desks. Jake no longer feels comfortable in his ability to de-escalate this situation alone but is unsure of what he should do next.*

COPS: LIBRARY EDITION

The relationship between libraries and the police may be one of the tensest topics in the profession. As discussed in Chapter 2, the values of law enforcement do not always align with the missions and values of libraries. Librarians value a right to privacy. Many police officers may just as well prefer limited or no privacy in public places. Libraries welcome diversity in all its forms. Some police departments appear very limited in this regard. It is not uncommon (as discussed in Chapter 2) for law enforcement to see library data as a treasure trove of insight about potential suspects, but librarians—like medical professionals—believe it is their duty to preserve the privacy of this data as much as legally possible. Both libraries and police serve an important role in enforcing and preserving constitutional rights, but they are more of a yin and yang—equal but opposing—than direct allies in serving this role.

A good deal of literature exists (including Chapter 2 of this book) on the USA PATRIOT Act, law enforcement interactions with libraries, and why their relationship may be less than friendly.[1] We will offer just a brief overview/refresher here. As a provision of the Uniting and Strengthening America by Providing Appropriate Tools to Restrict, Intercept and Obstruct Terrorism Act of 2001 (which is understandably often abbreviated to the acronym USA PATRIOT Act, and now referred to colloquially as the "Patriot Act"), law enforcement has broadly defined powers to collect information on individuals "suspected" (also broadly defined) of potentially engaging in criminal activity. Since the passage of the act (and, actually, many decades *before* its passage), there has been significant debate about law enforcement's right to access library data. Concern about the extent to which law enforcement may attempt to push and stretch enforcement of the PATRIOT Act has contributed to animosity among these groups.

Another significant concern is the profiling of library patrons and employees based on characteristics like appearance, language spoken, or the demographics of the community in which the library is located. This is likely to be the greater source of reluctance toward inviting police into the library during a conflict like that of Jake's. The history of the United States' public libraries illustrates the legitimacy of this concern. The age of Jim Crow laws and segregation of public libraries should not be forgotten, nor should the hidden and explicit racism and police brutality that persist today.[2] There is no straightforward solution to this concern. Indeed, as you will find in this chapter, advice on best practices is varied and contradictory. Each library and its stakeholders (patrons, employees, etc.) will be served to meet and develop an appropriate policy. The best we can do here is synthesize a bit of guidance on the matter.

This chapter focuses on two elements of law enforcement involvement in libraries. The first is the presence of law enforcement in and around the library as a preemptive measure to deter criminal activity. The second is what factors should be considered when calling on law enforcement to intervene in a hostile situation like that faced by Jake. There are two predominant forms of thought on these challenges, which often align with political and social perspectives of the authors/library administrators discussing them. This chapter will parse through the argument on both sides—and everything in between—to identify whether any room for compromise exists.

DO WE EVEN LET THEM IN?

After writing the initial draft of this chapter in 2019, it felt inadequate not to return to it in late 2020 and share what impact the events of this year had on how libraries have interacted with law enforcement. Following the murder of George Floyd, social justice protests, "defund the police," and sharp political divisions on the topic of policing, a rift has become clear (one that always existed) both in the general national discourse and among librarians. We found it impossible not to note how libraries and librarians have responded to these events, given the subject of these chapters. As always, we are interested only in "providing the facts" on what others have done, rather than suggest there is one right or wrong answer.

Particularly following the protests in late May and June 2020, many libraries and librarians felt compelled to reassess and/or make vocal their stance on libraries and police presence. Meredith Schwartz, editor of *Library Journal*, noted in July 2020 that, though it has traditionally been commonplace to see a police presence in libraries, whether it be off-duty cops moonlighting as security guards or the local police holding outreach events in the library's spaces, we must consider calling the police to be a last resort that is only used when it is impossible to handle situations with library employees alone.[3] Amanda Oliver reflected on her own experience with library police at the

D.C. Public Library, noting that, while the presence of these officers brought some comfort in certain situations, this experience was not shared by all members of the library staff.[4] She makes a passionate argument for reallocating resources dedicated to library security to areas like social work/workers. Cass Balzer and coauthors Jarrett Dapier and Emily Knox discuss why and how libraries can and should discontinue supporting the use of police within their facilities.[5] As Dapier and Knox note, "Police are not a de facto security service and should not be used in that way."[6] Only in the most unambiguously serious situations (e.g., shootings) should police be called.

A group of Ivy+ (an expanded group of "Ivy League" schools) librarians posted a call for reform in library–police relations in late October 2020. Seven statements were included in this call, to be addressed by libraries:

1. Support existing student, staff, faculty, and community petitions and movements (they provide examples, for instance, of student and faculty-led initiatives to sever ties between universities and local police).

2. Make transparent current police and police-like activities (this includes existing budgets and activities of these agencies).

3. Join, build, and sustain a world without policing (suggesting that libraries end reliance on law enforcement for addressing conflict by 2022).

4. Confront the connection between policing and anti-blackness.

5. Divest library resources from police and invest in our communities.

6. Ban surveillance technologies (and data collection) in library spaces.

7. Divest from companies that use prison labor.[7]

In at least one major case, a police department responded to a library's effort to support the Black Lives Matter movement. In late July 2020, a Lake Tahoe (Nevada) area sheriff sent a letter to the local library board, which was considering publishing a diversity statement that acknowledged the BLM movement, saying that if they did so, "please do not feel the need to call 911 for help."[8] The library's statement in question did not mention "defund the police" at all, instead reading as follows:

"We support #BlackLivesMatter. We resolutely assert and believe that all forms of racism, hatred, inequality, and injustice don't belong in our society."[9]

Ultimately, the library director and sheriff in this situation met to clarify their remarks, which they characterized as a "misunderstanding."

Some authors have noted that funding for libraries and funding for police appear linked in some circumstances. For instance, Elahi noted that the 2020 budget for the city of Louisville (KY) showed a $700,000 increase in the police budget for the fiscal year, while the library budget for the year decreased by that same amount.[10] While it was noted that the library said it approved the cut, some might question why a cut was made while police funding increased, when many were advocating for decreased police funding. In another article, by Daarel Burnette II, educators and librarians note that they have already been "defunded" for many years—not in the sense of a complete defunding but in the sense of small but frequent reductions and reallocations.[11] In their minds, why should the budgets of police forces not be reduced for a while to fill the educational funding gap? Again, the purpose of this book is not to advocate for any particular perspective on this issue, but to make readers aware that these perspectives exist so that they may make their own informed decisions.

Regardless of their personal perspectives on these issues relative to libraries, many libraries and librarians have felt that it is necessary to educate patrons about them. Seattle Central College and the University of Washington, among others, published LibGuides on the subject of Black Lives Matter, antiracism, and defund the police.[12] Stanford University Libraries organized an exhibition that featured the stories of victims of police brutality and systematic racism.[13] Amy Martin, in an article for *School Library Journal*, noted that the portrayals of police officers in picture books do not always match the reality for all children.[14] All of these efforts are a bit outside the scope of this book, but are worth mentioning given their relevance to the topic of libraries and police relations.

BALANCING PRIVACY AND SECURITY

In the early years of the first decade of the 2000s, the Alliance Library System of Illinois (now part of the Reaching Across Illinois Library System) published a detailed guide on library safety.[15] In this nearly 200-page document, which includes dozens of examples of policies and procedures used by Illinois libraries to ensure the safety of the library and its patrons, there are sections for "The Police," "Library Behavior Policies," and "Incident Reporting," among others. In the section entitled "The Police," the authors encourage developing a positive ongoing relationship with local police and sharing existing patron behavior policies with these officials so that they can best understand when and how they should intervene.[16] The authors suggest that the police have as much of a presence as possible, such as allowing them to teach programs on drug identification or have desks for officers to work within the library. Given the often fragmented relationship between law enforcement and library values, this suggestion by the Alliance Library System may not be well received by some readers. However, reaching some middle ground that improves communication and understanding of library policies may help in situations like that experienced by our library friend Jake.

Many public libraries have short, straightforward policies regarding calling the police for assistance. Franklin Public Library in Nebraska provides a list of inappropriate actions for library patrons (such as smoking, bringing pets into the library, or having sex in the library restroom) and provides the following four-step process for dealing with infractions:

1. Issue a verbal warning that if the behavior in question does not cease, the patron will be asked to leave the library premises

2. If unacceptable behavior continues, request that the patron leave the premises

3. If patron refuses to leave, inform him/her that the police will be called

4. Call the police

   - The policy provides the caveat that, if the individual engaging in the behavior is a minor, parents may be called instead of the police[17]

The Rainsville (AL) public library features a detailed policy for handling inappropriate behavior on its website, including an example of a "banning letter" that would be provided to a patron in the case that they engage in inappropriate behavior that is deemed worthy of a punishment including a temporary or permanent banishment from the library's premises and a corresponding appeal procedure.[18] This policy is particularly clear in illuminating the circumstances in which the police may be called to intervene in an incident in the library. Specifically, seven cases are listed (though other cases may be included if the library staff feel it's necessary for public safety):

1. Disruptive, harassing, or threatening behavior towards library users or staff

2. Making any threats of violence or unlawful behavior

3. Exhibiting any behavior that may be deemed as sexual harassment by library users or staff, including,

   a. sexual pranks or jokes

   b. verbal abuse of sexual nature

   c. repeatedly standing too close or brushing against a person

   d. repeatedly asking a person to meet or socialize outside of the library when they have said no

   e. Giving gifts that are sexually suggestive

   f. Repeatedly making sexually suggestive gestures

   g. Engaging in indecent exposure

4. Possessing, using, or selling illegal substances

5. Possessing, using, selling, or displaying a weapon

6. Trespassing after receiving a ban or during non-operating hours

7. Refusing to follow reasonable directions from library staff[19]

Of course, many libraries simply say (more or less), "follow the law or the cops get called." This may leave a high level of ambiguity that could cause concern for patrons, but in practice it is not different from the policy of almost every organization an individual enters (e.g., McDonald's, Walmart, City Hall).

Many of the public library policies regarding calling the police may be informed by the policies of the municipal government. For instance, the City of Portland (OR) lists its police procedures on its website (https://www.portlandoregon.gov/police/article/31583). Portland's public library would likely utilize this procedural document in developing its own policy for involving the police in a situation.

In academic libraries, policies pertaining to contacting police or security are often dictated at the university administration level. For instance, Penn State University has a fairly extensive policy section on "Managing Disruptions within the Library." This policy contains a specific section for the "role of University police" that explains that staff should contact campus police "if they or other library users feel threatened, if they suspect that some-one has committed acts of theft or vandalism, or if they have been instructed to do so by their supervisors or unit heads."[20] This policy is informed/under-scored by general student policies of the university, such as the "Student Guide to General University Policies and Rules" and "Penn State University Student Code of Conduct."

Michigan State University Libraries similarly bases their disruption inter-vention policy on general university policy.[21] In fact, the library's policy on calling the police is the university policy (the library policy simply references the university policy). The university policy refers to the following as exam-ples of disorderly conduct that may result in police being contacted to inter-vene: obstructing, hindering, or impeding the normal operations of any person, firm, or agency, or the use of property; obstructing, hindering, or impeding the normal operation of any class, laboratory, seminar, exam, field trip, or other educational activity (among other examples).[22]

The University of California at Santa Cruz lists three circumstances in which police may be contacted: trespassing (including when patrons refuse to leave the building after the time it is closed), any harassment (including sexual harassment), and violence/vandalism toward library property.[23] Many additional circumstances in which police may become involved in on-campus incidents are listed in the university student handbook.[24]

The University of Kansas does not have a specific outline for involving the police in incidents, except for in circumstances in which a weapon is brought into library property, but does outline very clearly policies for each area/service within the library, what is deemed appropriate/inappropriate, and how the situation might "escalate" if proper adherence is not followed.[25] A potential drawback of this thorough a policy is that it almost ensures that no library patron will actually read it; however, it does protect the library well in the case a patron wants to question the library's response to a situation. A simple solution is to have both a complete policy that clearly articulates the rules, like with the University of Kansas, but also a shorter, straightforward policy document that communicates basic procedures to library patrons. Call it the "Cliff Notes" version, if you like.

WHAT THE RESEARCH SAYS

In the realm of scholarly research and critical inquiry, there are many examples of guidance for working with law enforcement to curb disruptions in the library. Ben Robinson pushes back against suggestions like that of the Alliance Library System that libraries should strengthen relationships with law enforcement through increased cooperation and presence.[26] Robinson notes that research in many disciplines indicates that an increased police presence results in negative effects for individuals of an ethnic or sexual minority, people with a disability or mental illness, and members of other marginalized groups.

Robinson's perspective, however, is not the only one. Many scholars do indicate that a model like that presented by the Alliance Library Association may be useful for libraries. These advocates include Steve Albrecht, author of the book *Library Security*.[27] Albrecht is a retired reserve police sergeant with an educational background in security and business administration (though he is not a librarian). He suggests that engagement with local law enforcement (including law enforcement activities in the library) can be a practical way to build relationships that will benefit the library should law enforcement intervention be needed. Another similar book (also noted by Robinson in the article) is Warren Graham's *The Black Belt Librarian*.[28] Graham is a former security manager for several public libraries in North Carolina. He is able to draw on his firsthand experience often in his writing. As with Albrecht, Graham supports the building of a strong relationship with security/law enforcement.

An ideal situation for some libraries may seemingly be to hire a security guard, which conveys that inappropriate behavior will not be tolerated, but this may not cause the same negative emotional effect in some patrons. However, as Robinson notes, even security guards may provoke negative emotions, particularly as many guards do not receive any significant sensitivity training and may be more likely to bring unprofessional prejudices and behaviors onto the job with them. Perhaps even more problematic is simply that most libraries cannot afford to hire security personnel. A small public library is unlikely to have a funds to hire a new employee (and if they did, it would likely be another librarian rather than a security guard).

So, in the absence of increased security or police presence in the library, what would authors like Robinson recommend be done? Robinson suggests that the root challenges that result in criminal activity be targeted. By working with social workers or providing trainings to library employees so that they can "become" social workers, Robinson suggests, incidents like that experienced by Jake can be prevented. Of course, this policy does not give us much advice on what to do when a problematic situation like Jake's does arise. It is likely that those whose thoughts align with Robinson's would only want to call on the cops to intervene as a very last resort, not just because of the effect on the parties directly involved, but also on other patrons who use the library in lawful ways. Pushing library employees to the ground may be the point where the need for police intervention would seem obvious.

GUIDANCE FROM OTHER DISCIPLINES

Traditionally, the presence of a security guard in a museum is by no means an unexpected sight. To the contrary, in some art museums, security seemingly outnumbers patrons at times. However, like with the discussion here, the role of security guards in museums has not gone unchallenged, particularly in recent times. Prominent social science thinkers like Tony Bennett, working from the perspective of power/knowledge/control theories associated with Marx, Gramsci, and Foucault, among others, suggest that museums have historically been places designed to support cultural hegemony and control and that the presence of security guards is one way in which the distance between the viewer and the art is established and maintained (in simplified terms: *you can look at this art, but you cannot really be intimate with it or truly understand it, nor even earn our trust that you will observe it properly, because you are common folk*).[29] What effect might be anticipated if libraries had security guards patrol like at museums? Would patrons be willing to pick up a book from the stacks, or would they be too nervous about doing something wrong and being punished by a guard? What effect would this have on library anxiety, when patrons are already nervous about interacting with a librarian?

Seemingly, this increased security presence may suggest that patrons in this library are not trusted—particularly when the presence did not exist before—and seems as though it might invite profiling of library patron populations, such that libraries in the suburbs may have a lower security presence than libraries in certain areas of the city.

One of the most widely noted areas in which police presence has increased in recent decades is in schools. There is an extensive data trail for the effectiveness (or lack thereof) of these programs. Many of these studies have indicated that increased police presence has been ineffective in reducing future crime, and some, like Na and Gottfredson, indicate that increased police presence has resulted in greater reports of nonserious crimes while failing to reduce the incidence of serious crimes.[30] Importantly, Arrick Jackson, among others, found that police presence has no effect on students' perceptions of police or committing crimes.[31] Conversely, some researchers, like Theriot, indicate that the presence of a school resource officer does decrease the prevalence of assault and weapons offenses.[32] The overall findings for the effectiveness of increased police presence in schools is, at best, murky.

The measurable effect that police presence may have in museums, schools, and libraries is in increasing the comfort level of some patrons that crime is less likely to occur, even if this is not true. This is the same principle that security at public events and the TSA at airports largely serves—if somebody wanted to commit a crime in any of those places, they could, but seeing the security guard gives everyone peace of mind. Zhao, Schneider, and Thurman, in a systematic analysis of literature related to the effect of police presence on the public's emotions, found that police presence has a "strong impact" on public fear reduction.[33] However, findings by Hinkle and Weisburd suggest that this effect is dependent on demographic factors, including race, where those who identified as Black experienced heightened distress with increased police presence in public.[34]

OUR GUIDANCE

Some might wonder, "If I am putting a policy together, how should I go about it? Should I involve the police in the development of the policy?" There is not a lot of guidance available on this topic, unlike other aspects of security and privacy that are better defined. The answer has become even less clear in the wake of the events and movements in 2020. Many libraries still maintain strong ties to police and security; others have nearly completely dissolved what relationships existed.

Libraries must consider their unique situation to determine what is appropriate. If a new policy is needed, consider who the key stakeholders should be: staff, patrons, community leaders, BLM leaders. While it may be worthwhile to receive input from local law enforcement about the library's policy, they probably should be involved in actually drafting the library's policy given their "closeness" to the issue.

This may also be an area where policy is actually not needed at all. If a library decides that the only time that law enforcement will be contacted is when a suspected crime has occurred, then a policy may not be necessary (essentially, the "policy" is the law). The times where a clear policy may be needed are when the library intends to use police to intervene in situations that are problematic/disruptive but do not really reach the point of being criminal (such as a heated argument between two patrons).

So, in the case of Jake, what should be done? Considering that Jake was pushed to the floor—which is assault—a potential crime occurred, which is a clear cause for police involvement. Now, if the two patrons were just arguing and Jake had not been pushed to the floor? There could be more of a gray area. It is not a crime to argue (however, it is a crime to trespass, in the case that the patrons are breaking library rules and are no longer welcome inside). Given the tensions in the United States, it may be that the library staff does everything in its power not to call the cops—up to and including threatening to do so.

Another solution may be to identify one librarian on staff who can serve as a "security liaison." This person might have a background in social work and security intervention strategies, while also being a professional librarian and understanding the professional ethics and values of the field. This "security guard librarian" would be responsible for intervening in these types of problematic situations, as a security officer typically would. They would, however, have a much better understanding of the concerns of library staff and patrons than a traditional security officer does. This individual would be more attuned to the "philosophy of librarianship" while having the outward authority of a security officer. This may be both more economical (instead of hiring security guards as a separate paid position) and better PR for the library (though we are not suggesting that it is the only—or best—solution).

As with all guidance in this book, best practices can vary from jurisdiction to jurisdiction. Readers in Australia, for instance, might find guidance from ALIA more valuable than that from ALA. The Australian Library and Information Association provides guidelines pertaining to police interaction with libraries that is applicable both to this chapter and to Chapter 2.[35] The Chartered Institute of Library and Information Professionals (CILIP) in the United Kingdom has its own policies related to involvement with police, based on law in that region.

CONCLUSION

On the surface, calling the police to intervene when a fight or other problematic event occurs may seem like a straightforward idea to some. However, it may be argued that this is a privileged position to take, and that for many library users, a positive relationship with the police is not to be expected. While this is not to suggest that the police should unilaterally not be trusted, or certainly that they should not be contacted if truly needed, it is to suggest that, if a matter can be handled in-house, intervention by library staff will likely result in less anxiety, anger, and frustration than intervention by police. This may be particularly true for some libraries more than others, so libraries, as always, should do their best to understand their patrons and what response will cause the least amount of distress to them.

Increased police presence in libraries, even having space for police officers to work within the library as suggested by Graham and Albrecht, may be a helpful idea for some libraries. But, as suggested in the literature of museum studies and education, research has shown that the presence of law enforcement in an area does not necessarily reduce the incidence of crime and often results in nonserious offenses (that could probably be handled by the library staff) being pursued and punished as though they were serious crimes. Again, actions like this may actually increase distrust among library patrons toward the police, rather than spawning positive interactions. These relationships must, therefore, be pursued cautiously and carefully. As always, discourse between the library and its service population may support best practices in this matter.

NOTES

1. Karl T. Gruben, "What is Johnny doing in the library: Libraries, the USA PATRIOT Act, and its amendments," *St. Thomas Law Review* 19, no. 2 (2006): 299–331; Paul T. Jaeger, Charles R. McClure, John Carlo Bertot, and John T. Snead, "The USA PATRIOT Act, the Foreign Intelligence Surveillance Act, and information policy research in libraries: Issues, impacts, and questions for libraries and researchers," *Library Quarterly* 74, no. 2 (2004): 99–121; Chris Matz, "Libraries and the USA PATRIOT Act: Values in conflict," *Journal of Library Administration* 47, no. 3/4 (2008): 68–87; Heather A. Phillips, "Libraries and national security law: An examination of the USA PATRIOT Act," *Progressive Librarian* 25 (2005): 28–42.

2. Cheryl Knott, *Not free, not for all: Public libraries in the age of Jim Crow* (Amherst: University of Massachusetts Press, 2016); Cheryl K. Malone, "Toward a multicultural American public library history," *Libraries and Culture* 35, no. 1

(2000): 77–87; Lorna Peterson, "Alternative perspectives in library and information science: Issues of race," *Journal of Education for Library and Information Science* 37, no. 2 (1996): 163–174.

3. Meredith Schwartz, "Make the right call," *Library Journal*, retrieved July 6, 2020. https://www.libraryjournal.com/?detailStory=make-the-right-call -editorial

4. Amanda Oliver, *Racism, violence, and police in our public libraries*, retrieved June 8, 2020. https://aelaineo.medium.com/racism-violence-and-police -in-our-public-libraries-cd3983ac6044

5. Cass Balzer, "Rethinking police presence," *American Libraries*, retrieved July 8, 2020. https://americanlibrariesmagazine.org/2020/07/08/rethinking -police-presence

6. Jarrett Dapier and Emily Knox, "When not to call the cops," *American Libraries*, retrieved July 8, 2020. https://americanlibrariesmagazine.org/2020 /07/08/rethinking-when-to-call-the-cops/

7. Abolitionist Library Association Ivy+, *A call for Ivy+ libraries to divest from police and prisons and invest in life-giving resources*, retrieved October 28, 2020. https://ablaivy.medium.com/a-call-for-ivy-libraries-to-divest-from-police -and-prisons-and-invest-in-life-giving-resources-fdd5889270df

8. Anna Bauman, *Nevada sheriff to library supporting Black Lives Matter: "Do not feel the need to call 911,"* retrieved July 30, 2020. https://www.police1. com/chiefs-sheriffs/articles/nev-sheriff-to-library-supporting-blm-do-not-feel -the-need-to-call-911-PsIcdPQS4U4AZaZq

9. Ibid.

10. Amina Elahi, "Louisville budget maintaining police funding passes with broad support," *WFPL Louisville*, retrieved June 25, 2020. https://wfpl.org /louisville-budget-maintaining-police-funding-passes-with-broad-support

11. Daarel Burnette II, "Schools or police: In some cities, a reckoning on spending priorities," *Education Week*, retrieved June 18, 2020. https://www .edweek.org/leadership/schools-or-police-in-some-cities-a-reckoning-on -spending-priorities/2020/06

12. Seattle Central College, *Safety while protesting: Research on police brutality and abolition*, retrieved November 3, 2020. https://libguides.seattlecentral .edu/c.php?g=1046607&p=7594343; University of Washington, *Racial justice resources: Defund the police*, retrieved December 15, 2020. https://guides.lib .uw.edu/racial-justice/defundpolice

13. Gabrielle Karampelas, *The Say Their Names—No More Names exhibition opens at Stanford Libraries*, retrieved September 4, 2020. https://news.stanford. edu/2020/09/04/say-names-no-names-exhibit-stanford-libraries

14. Amy Martin, "Too good to be true? Picture book portrayals of police officers don't reflect everyone's reality," *School Library Journal*, retrieved June 2,

2020. https://www.slj.com/?detailStory=Police-Picture-Books-Revisited-the-Lie-White-Adults-Read-to-Children-opinion

15. Rose M. Chenoweth et al., *Policies and procedures for a safe library*, Alliance Library System (n.d.). https://library.wyo.gov/downloads/ldo/pdf/boards/SafeWorkplace.pdf

16. Ibid., 19.

17. Franklin Public Library, *Public behavior, safety, and emergency policy*, retrieved July 1, 2019. http://libraries.ne.gov/franklin/files/2016/08/Public-Behavior-Safety-and-Emergency-Policy-1.pdf

18. Rainsville Public Library, *Rainsville Public Library policies and procedures*, retrieved August 3, 2019. https://www.rainsvillepubliclibrary.com/library-policies--procedures.html

19. Ibid.

20. Pennsylvania State University Libraries, *Policies and guidelines*, retrieved March 11, 2020. https://libraries.psu.edu/policies/u/-adg/2

21. Michigan State University Libraries, *Library disruptions*, retrieved March 10, 2020. https://lib.msu.edu/about/policy-disruptions

22. Michigan State University, *15.00 disorderly assemblages or conduct*, retrieved October 21, 2019. https://trustees.msu.edu/bylaws-ordinances-policies/ordinances/ordinance-15.00.html

23. University of California Santa Cruz, *University library policies*, February 25, 2020. https://library.ucsc.edu/about/university-library-policies

24. Regents of the University of California, *Student handbook & university policies*, retrieved January 18, 2020. https://deanofstudents.ucsc.edu/student-conduct/student-handbook/index.html

25. University of Kansas, *Library policies and procedures*, retrieved July 16, 2019. https://lib.ku.edu/policies

26. Ben Robinson, *No holds barred: Policing and security in the public library*, In the Library with the Lead Pipe, retrieved December 11, 2019. http://www.inthelibrarywiththeleadpipe.org/2019/no-holds-barred

27. Steve Albrecht, *Library security: Better communication, safer facilities* (Chicago, IL: American Library Association, 2015).

28. Warren Graham, *The black belt librarian* (Chicago, IL: American Library Association, 2011).

29. Tony Bennett, *The birth of the museum* (London, UK: Routledge, 1995).

30. Kevin P. Brady, Sharon Balmer, and Deinya Phenix, "School-police partnership effectiveness in urban schools," *Education and Urban Society* 39, no. 4 (2007): 455–478; Mario S. Torres and Jacqueline A. Stefkovich, "Demographics and police involvement: Implications for student civil liberties and just leadership," *Educational Administration Quarterly* 45, no. 3 (2009): 450–473; Chongmin Na and Denise C. Gottfredson, "Police officers in schools: Effects on school

crime and the processing of offending behaviors," *Justice Quarterly* 30, no. 4 (2013): 619–650.

31. Arrick Jackson, "Police-school resource officers' and students' perceptions of the police and offending," *Policing* 25, no. 3 (2002): 631–650.

32. Matthew T. Theriot, "School resource officers and the criminalization of student behavior," *Journal of Criminal Justice* 37, no. 3 (2009): 280–287.

33. Jihong Zhao, Matthew Schneider, and Quint Thurman, "The effect of police presence on public fear reduction and satisfaction: A review of the literature," *Justice Professional* 15, no. 3 (2002): 273–299.

34. Joshua C. Hinkle and David Weisburd, "The irony of broken windows policing: A micro-place study of the relationship between disorder, focused police crackdowns and fear of crime," *Journal of Criminal Justice* 36, no. 6 (2008): 503–512.

35. Australian Library and Information Association, *Library and privacy guidelines*, retrieved November 15, 2019. https://www.alia.org.au/about-alia /policies-and-guidelines/alia-policies/libraries-and-privacy-guidelines

PART II

Libraries and Basic Computer Privacy

Many books on library privacy focus on what things *are*, but not what to *do* about them. What is the point of that? "Glad I paid $65 for a book with some interesting facts I can do nothing with!" In Part II of this book, we want to take on a little different philosophy. Here we point out some common library computer privacy challenges and then discuss how, from policy down to practice, we can face these challenges with confidence. We also prepare for when those unforeseen circumstances in life throw everything askew, as we discuss how to keep privacy in mind while transitioning to remote library services.

FIVE

Looking over Your Shoulder (Literally and Figuratively)

Rose is a reference librarian at the main branch of a large academic library system. Part of her job as a reference librarian is to meander through the library to see if any patrons need any assistance (e.g., mobile reference). As she walked down a row of computer terminals one day, she passed by two students, one of whom was accessing their school enrollment records while the other, sitting a bit behind her and off to the side, watched. Rose kept walking.

Shortly afterward, the student using the computer to access their enrollment record approached the reference desk to ask for assistance with printing a document. As Rose was assisting this student, she offhandedly remarked, "so was that your friend that was sitting with you earlier?" The student responded that she had no idea anyone was sitting near her, and when Rose described the person, the student said she had never before met such a person. Glancing around the room, Rose identified the "friend" as they walked toward the library exit. Internally, she debated whether to shout at the individual or report the incident to library administration or campus police.

THE DARK-HOODED FIGURE OF YOUR NIGHTMARES

When we talk of criminals and surveillance, many people likely envision a figure in a dark hoodie that stalks prey in the darkness. It would be misleading to say that such figures do not exist at all, but it is equally likely that the person who envisions your information as prey looks like a "regular Joe." It may even be someone you know, like a classmate or coworker. So do not ever let your guard down (but also do not let fear run your life!). Most people are not looking to steal your information, but some are and it is always better to be safe than sorry.

This chapter, like many chapters throughout this book, synthesizes literature on two interrelated topics. The first is security practices when using public computers and spaces. Since library employees can be victims of this surveillance, whether physical surveillance by individuals or electronic surveillance by online entities, in addition to the patrons they serve, it is important for them to understand and be able to instruct patrons on basic security practice. The second is what libraries should do if patrons are observed to be spying on the activities of others.

SOME SECURITY THREATS

There are many, many resources that discuss computers in libraries—in fact, there is an entire conference and periodical ("Computers in Libraries") dedicated to it—and computer privacy, so we will not spend too long discussing the topic. However, it does seem necessary to provide a short, focused review of the topic and best practices as a computer user to ensure the security of your data. Several of the concepts introduced here will be discussed in greater detail in following chapters.

Types of Computer Data That Threaten User Privacy

IP Address

Each Internet-connected device has a unique Internet Protocol (IP) address, which, like with a mailing address, tells others (like a server/website with which you want to connect) "where" you are (as in, what device is being used). An IP address is required for connecting to the Internet, like a mailing address is required if you want to receive mail. However, as this IP information is transferred on the web, it can be acquired by others for whom it was not intended. In fact, this collection occurs quite frequently and without the user's knowledge. If you have ever filled in a web form, there is a good chance that your IP address and location data were collected without your knowledge.

Website Client Information

When you access a website, that site receives not only information provided by your IP address, but also information about your behavior on the website and other sites that you have visited (these packets of information that follow from site-to-site are called "cookies" but are not very tasty).

Knowledge of users' online behavior is useful to websites and companies in the same way that knowledge of the information behavior of library users is useful to libraries. If we know what people do and want, we can better provide it to them. Of course, the central difference is that libraries simply want to provide better service, while websites generally use this knowledge for purposes like the marketing of specific items or ideas, or even the sale or exchange of data with others.

Fingerprinting

When a computer accesses a website, it transmits the IP address, any cookies, and session information, but also a host of other types of information, all of which can be used to identify the computer and in some instances the person using it. This process is called "fingerprinting." A typical fingerprint of a user using a computer includes the IP address, any cookies, but also the browser the person is using and its version. Other information transmitted includes the operating system they are using, its version, screen resolution, the type of device that is being used, and so on. Even though each individual piece of this fingerprint is not identifying, putting them all together into a single "fingerprint" *can* be identifying. Using the fingerprint, someone could track or follow someone or a device across the Internet.

Use of Public Computers

Public computers, such as those provided by libraries, are often utilized by multiple unique users on any given day. The data one accesses, stores, and uses on these computers can potentially be accessed by subsequent users, as copies of this data may have been locally stored on the computer. This is particularly risky, of course, if the computer does not require log-in credentials to access certain privacy and storage features.

Search Engines and the Filter Bubble

Search engines are a business, and very big business at that. In 2019, Google made nearly $100 billion in advertising revenue, largely from two platforms: YouTube and the Google Search.[1] The history of Google is fascinating, particularly because of the search engine's foundations in information science research, including principles of informetrics/citation analysis that underpin Google's PageRank methodology. However, unlike libraries that use these research principles to improve services for the public at no direct cost,

Google and other search engines do the same but with profit motives in mind. By threading relevant ads into users' search results, search engines drive millions of clicks to third-party sites each day. By continuously curating search results based on prior search behavior, results are often more relevant and drive more clicks, but searchers are exposed to less diverse/differing viewpoints on a topic. They are put in a "bubble" where their information world is increasingly narrowed based on past behavior.

Web Browsers and Search History

All web browsers locally store information for some length of time, so that users can easily navigate "back" to a page they previously visited. Some browsers (Internet Explorer, Google Chrome) store this information indefinitely unless deleted by the user. Others (Tor, Brave) may delete the browsing history after each session. When using a personal password-protected computer, maintaining your browsing history can be a helpful way to return to regularly visited websites. However, when using a public or shared computer, the storage of browsing history by the browser poses significant harm to users' privacy.

Another Example

The New York Public Library provides a convenient page on its website where it describes all the data that is collected from visitors to its site, so it makes for a nice little example of just how much data about you—the web user—is out there and acquired by each site you visit. You can check it out at this archived link: http://web.archive.org/web/20200415003648/https://www.nypl.org/help/about-nypl/legal-notices/privacy-policy. Here is the data that is collected just when you visit the NYPL site (before logging in):

- Your Internet Protocol (IP) address
- Your location
- Kind of web browser or electronic device that you use
- Date and time of your visit
- Website that you visited immediately before arriving at our website
- Pages that you viewed on our website
- Certain searches/queries that you conducted[2]

We are not saying that the New York Public Library will use your data to do harm, but we are saying that it does have your data, as do most other sites you visit, including ones that might not be quite a trustworthy as the NYPL. With this data they collect, it is possible to develop an entire map (like something out of *The Dark Knight*) that shows where and when people are accessing the New York Public Library's website. So, while you do not have to be superstitious about how this basic data is used, you may want to be at least a little stitious.

WHAT LIBRARIES SAY

Starting at the top, so to speak, the American Library Association has a set of guidelines for public access computers and networks.[3] The guidelines are succinct but include all the details you need in order to know the ALA's perspective on providing privacy on public access computers. If sign-in sheets are used (which, in theory, may not be a bad idea to catch that spy from Rose's example), the ALA guidelines suggest this sheet be destroyed when no longer needed. They also suggest that privacy screens be made available to patrons if they wish to use one (these are discussed more in the "Our Guidance" section). They recommend that all browsers be configured to clear user data on exit and that any files stored on a device be deleted when the patron is finished using it. Regular maintenance to upgrade malware detection/antivirus software is also suggested. There is a companion checklist for these guidelines, which prioritizes the implementation of these privacy measures.[4]

While the San Francisco Public Library's privacy policies are not discussed elsewhere in this book, they should be commended as a whole for their breadth and clarity.[5] Not only do they outline a response to virtually every ethical privacy dilemma raised in this book, they also provide a library patron privacy inventory that lists what types of data will be collected from patrons for which library services as well as a detailed Frequently Asked Questions document about patron privacy. In the patron privacy inventory, patrons can find information about how browser data will be stored—it will be deleted as soon as the patron logs off or time elapses and the computer automatically reboots—and patron lending records deleted once the item lent is returned. The FAQ document includes information about California's specific information privacy laws (which are very progressive and worth looking at for privacy policy advocates), the USA PATRIOT Act, and specific rules within the library. Here, the document explicitly states that "the Library's public computer stations are programmed to delete the history of a library user's Internet session and all searches once an individual session is completed."[6]

The San Jose Public Library has similar policies in place.[7] Browsing history is deleted when the patron finishes their use of the computer. However, San Jose does collect a bit of anonymized data about computer usage—not the content that is accessed but just what computers were used and for what length of time. These statistics can be helpful in advocating for more computer terminals, for example, and as long as the data collection is anonymous and can be justified (there is a good reason to collect it), then it is unlikely to raise the concern of patrons. The San Jose Public Library also conducts regular privacy audits to ensure that different aspects of their operation align with their privacy policy.

Many public libraries simply appeal to state and federal privacy laws. These laws, however, pertain more to the storage and privacy of library records (checkouts, library card information, etc.) than use of public access computers. For this reason, it is important to have separate privacy policies for data that the library collects and data that may be collected by websites when using library computers. The former discusses what the library will not do (e.g., not share your information with anyone unless a legal order demands it), while the latter discusses what the library will do (e.g., set browser to delete all browsing history on closing).

The University of California-Berkeley Library's policy states that no personally identifiable information is collected from users of the library's website or public access computers.[8] "Cookies" collected on library computers are erased daily along with any browser data. In addition, the policy reiterates that any personal information shared with the library, electronically or otherwise, is considered confidential and will only be shared when compelled by legal order. The University of Washington Libraries has similar policies, with a few minor edits to comply with campus-wide privacy policy.[9] Specifically, the University of Washington has its own administrative policy for any data collected on its website or electronic services.[10]

As with public libraries, many academic libraries lack a publicly available computer privacy policy. The "computer use" policies that do exist dictate more what users cannot do rather than what they can. For instance, the Drake University computer use policy mentions that User ID and password are used to preserve the privacy of users, but otherwise only specifies the behaviors of patrons, such as that they should not use the library computers to conduct criminal activities, download unauthorized software, or engage in disruptive behavior.[11] This is a common phenomenon among academic libraries, as opposed to detailed privacy policies akin to the San Francisco Public Library's.

WHAT RESEARCHERS SAY

Trina Magi makes an important observation about library patron privacy when using vendor services.[12] Magi found that 24 of 27 library vendors had a privacy statement describing how user data is collected and used; however, many of the policies were not easy to find on the website and did not supply a "last updated" date. None of the vendors mention the ALA Code of Ethics or privacy guidelines. Ultimately, Magi concludes that most of the vendor privacy policies do not live up to the expectation of libraries and library users.

Hess, LaPorte-Fiori, and Engwall provide a discussion of how their library at Oakland University developed a public statement on patron privacy, which discusses data collection and destruction procedures.[13] Unsurprisingly, the authors took an approach that is the foundation of this book—evidence-based practice, informing their own statement from the successful statements utilized by other universities. As these authors note, not all aspects of library technology can be considered "secure" or "private," such as products by library vendors, as discussed in the Magi study.[14] In these situations, it is important to note that complete privacy cannot be guaranteed and to provide contact information for an individual who can answer questions about any privacy concerns.

An interesting area of study (which may be considered a subset of information behavior research) is information privacy behavior research. This area of research provides insight into the privacy practices in which an individual is likely to engage by their own volition (such as the likelihood that an individual would naturally delete their browser history on a public computer when they are finished using it). Schofield, Reips, Stieger, Joinson, and Buchanan; Debatin, Lovejoy, Horn, and Hughes; and LaRose and Rifon, for example, all found, to varying extent, that Internet users claim to have a good knowledge of privacy threats and practices they can use to mitigate these threats, but their behavior rarely demonstrates application of this knowledge.[15] Debatin et al., for instance, found that Facebook users claimed a high awareness of privacy issues and risks on the platform; however, they observed that large amounts of personal information were nonetheless shared on Facebook by these users' accounts.[16] This research appears to indicate that, even given knowledge of privacy risks, users are unlikely to take measures to ensure privacy.

McDonald and Cranor provide some compelling insight into users' beliefs and practices in regard to the collection of "cookies" and their usage in direct marketing.[17] The researchers found that 64 percent of users considered the use of cookies and other user data to support targeted advertising invasive or unwanted, compared to only 20 percent who indicated appreciation for the benefits of this collection and service. In addition, 40 percent said they would change their online behavior if they were aware that advertisers were tracking them (though few actually do it). Particularly opposed by respondents was the idea of advertisers having access to email content and using this data to develop advertising. About 91 percent of individuals surveyed by McDonald and Cranor thought this was an unacceptable idea.[18] In the United Kingdom,

Sutlieff and Chelin found a similar desire for privacy and a distrust for the collection and ownership of data among patrons of academic libraries.[19] Specifically, the researchers examined trust and beliefs in the National Identity Card Scheme (NICS), which was intended to provide a biographically and biometric-based identification system that could improve security against identity theft and make it easier for libraries to verify identity and loan items. However, this concept was met with great opposition from individuals (and particularly young adults) concerned with the privacy implications of the government having and using these types of data about its citizens. Zimmer found that 97 percent of librarian respondents to a survey about librarian attitudes about privacy indicated that personal information should never be shared outside of the library system.[20] This demonstrates that librarians are well aware of this concern, highlighted by McDonald and Cranor as well as Sutlieff and Chelin, about unwanted collection of user data.[21]

So Internet users consistently say that they want their privacy; they also say they have a pretty good idea of how to get it, but few actually implement change to improve their privacy. That is not surprising—we authors would probably admit the same, at least in regard to a few online privacy behaviors— but what does it mean for libraries? Arguably, it may mean that libraries, in light of the knowledge that patrons do indeed want privacy but do not necessarily want to work hard to get it, should make privacy features on public access computers as automated as possible, by setting browsers to delete data on exit, removing all data on logout, and providing privacy barriers or screen for the computers that are easily available rather than hidden behind some employee's desk. Information seekers are already focused on their task at hand; privacy should be something that they can take for granted while in the library environment.

OUR GUIDANCE

Much of the guidance we would suggest for the basic computer security concerns discussed in this chapter is inspired by prior work.[22] However, in this case, the guidance will be more general in order to avoid the information falling out of relevance within only a short few years. The most basic guidance we would offer is to set any browsers to delete browsing history on exit. Regardless of what browser you use (though we would recommend Brave or Tor, discussed in Chapter 9), the option to delete browser history on exit will be found in the browser settings, which is generally represented by a button on the left or right side of the top ribbon of the browser (the same menu where you can view bookmarks, print, etc.).

To reduce the extent to which IP address information can be collected, using a "dark web" network like Tor (again, discussed in Chapter 9) can be an excellent solution. However, in the absence of this solution, simply using care when sharing information online or when visiting suspicious websites can go a long way. This includes when participating in surveys—whether for academic research or otherwise. Look for the rationale for the survey—how do they say your data will be used?—and the practices the researchers will use to secure your data—does it say in the statement of informed consent? Anytime you share an email address or create an account on a website, ask yourself, "do I trust this site?" and "is this account really necessary/will I use it?" Do not create an account on sites just to create them—they are just another place where your data can potentially be compromised.

For the specific challenge faced by Rose, the best response may be to adjust the physical layout of the computer terminals within the library. Commonly, computers within a library are arranged in rows, with one computer next to another and/or one computer stationed in a row behind another, such that it makes it very easy to look over one's shoulder. If the physical arrangement cannot be changed, another simple, but potentially pricey, solution is privacy screens designed for computer monitors. These are flexible, tinted screens that are attached to a computer monitor and allow light to pass through only straight-on (for the user viewing the screen) but not from an angle (as how someone would look over that user's shoulder). These screens tend to cost a bit of money but are likely to be affordable given a small grant or other type of funding (as of 2020, they run about $35 each from most sources). Another option to lower costs (which seems to be supported in the ALA guidelines) is to make the privacy screens available for users but not required for every computer; this would mean that the library would not be on the hook for purchasing a privacy screen for every computer.

In the absence of a screen (which has some drawbacks, such as tinting the screen for the user) or physically rearranging computer spaces, it may be possible to create some level of privacy by placing barriers between computer stations. In a pinch, a large piece of cardboard could suffice. These barriers would prevent individuals at the stations directly adjacent (to the left and right) of the user from viewing what the user is doing, but would allow individuals to view from behind the user. Frankly, this may be a more amenable solution than some of the others discussed in this chapter for some libraries, as it would allow library employees to still walk through and monitor activity on computers while blocking other users from seeing. However, we encourage this solution only if the others (physical rearrangement, tinted screens) are not possible.

Conduct Your Own Privacy Audit

According to Merriam-Webster dictionary (yes, we went to the old "according to x . . ." formula), an audit is "a methodological examination or review."[23] The key word here is "methodological," which here may be considered a synonym for "carefully planned and structured." A privacy audit, then, is a "carefully planned and structured review of privacy," specifically, the privacy provided to patrons at your library. How does a privacy audit work? Like with a research project, the best place to start might be with the end product you want to achieve—What are your research questions? What do you want to learn? What do you want to do with it?

For example, your research question might be "is the library actually providing the types of privacy we say we will in our privacy policy?" One product you might want to develop from your findings is a library patron privacy inventory like the one from the San Francisco Public Library that informs patrons of what data is collected when and where, how long and where the data will be stored, and how the data may be used.[24] Now that you have a goal in mind, develop the audit accordingly. Plan to go department-to-department throughout the library, checking to see how well policy is enforced and how the "framework" of policy is implemented in the practice of daily procedures. Develop a straightforward inventory of what data is collected from patrons and what is done with it, and then make this inventory readily accessible to all.

CONCLUSION

Patron privacy while using library computers should be considered the responsibility of the library itself. A failure to educate users about privacy practices is a failure to protect patrons from significant threats they face with the library's walls. This chapter outlines some basic privacy practices that may be used to inform user privacy education, as well as guidance to inform policies and procedures about spying on another user's library usage. Each of the following chapters continues to delve a bit deeper into different aspects of online privacy and security for library patrons.

NOTES

1. Troy Wolverton, *Alphabet breaks out YouTube and Cloud financials for the first time as Google's overall revenue slowdown misses street targets*, retrieved February 3, 2020. https://www.businessinsider.com/alphabet-google-q4-2019 -earnings-search-ads-youtube-google-cloud-2020-2

2. New York Public Library, *The New York Public Library privacy policy*, retrieved March 30, 2020. http://web.archive.org/web/20200415003648/https://www.nypl.org/help/about-nypl/legal-notices/privacy-policy

3. American Library Association, *Library privacy guidelines for public access computers and networks*, retrieved March 4, 2020. http://www.ala.org/advocacy/privacy/guidelines/public-access-computer

4. American Library Association, *Library privacy checklist for public access computers and networks*, retrieved February 29, 2020. http://www.ala.org/advocacy/privacy/checklists/public-access-computer

5. San Francisco Public Library, *Privacy policy*, retrieved January 14, 2020. https://sfpl.org/about-us/privacy-policy

6. San Francisco Public Library, *Patron privacy frequently asked questions*, retrieved January 14, 2020. https://sfpl.org/sites/default/files/pdf/about/administration/privacypolicyfaq.pdf

7. San Jose Public Library, *Privacy policy*, retrieved December 29, 2019. https://www.sjpl.org/privacy-policy

8. University of California-Berkeley, *Collection, use, and disclosure of electronic information*, retrieved December 22, 2019. https://www.lib.berkeley.edu/about/privacy-electronic-information

9. University of Washington Libraries, *Privacy statement*, retrieved January 4, 2020. https://www.lib.washington.edu/about/policy/privacy

10. University of Washington, *Administrative policy statement: University privacy policy*, retrieved January 1, 2020. http://www.washington.edu/admin/rules/policies/APS/02.02.html

11. Drake University, *Computer use policy*, retrieved January 14, 2020. https://library.drake.edu/about-us/policies/public-use-of-computers

12. Trina J. Magi, "A content analysis of library vendor privacy policies: Do they meet our standards?" *College and Research Libraries* 71, no. 3 (2010): 254–272.

13. Amanda N. Hess, Rachelle LaPorte-Fiori, and Keith Engwall, "Preserving patron privacy in the 21st century academic library," *Journal of Academic Librarianship* 41, no. 1 (2015): 105–114.

14. Magi, "A content analysis of library vendor privacy policies."

15. Carina Paine Schofield, Ulf-Dietrich Reips, Stefan Stieger, Adam N. Joinson, and Tom Buchanan, "Internet users' perceptions of 'privacy concerns' and 'privacy actions.'" *International Journal of Human-Computer Studies* 65, no. 6 (2007): 526–536; Bernhard Debatin, Jennette P. Lovejoy, Ann-Kathrin Horn, and Brittany N. Hughes, "Facebook and online privacy: Attitudes, behaviors, and unintended consequences," *Journal of Computer-Mediated Communication* 15, no. 1 (2009): 83–108; Robert LaRose and Nora J Rifon, "Promoting i-safety:

Effects of privacy warnings and privacy seals on risk assessment and online privacy behavior," *Journal of Consumer Affairs* 41, no. 1 (2007): 127–149.

16. Debatin, "Facebook and online privacy."

17. Aleecia M. McDonald and Lorrie Faith Cranor, "Beliefs and behaviors: Internet users' understanding of behavioral advertising," *38th Research Conference on Communication, Information and Internet Policy* (2010). http://aleecia .com/authors-drafts/tprc-behav-AV.pdf

18. Ibid.

19. Lisa Sutlieff and Jackie Chelin, "An absolute prerequisite: The importance of user privacy and trust in maintaining academic freedom at the library," *Journal of Librarianship and Information Science* 42, no. 3 (2010): 163–177.

20. Michael Zimmer, "Librarians' attitudes regarding information and Internet privacy," *Library Quarterly: Information, Community, Policy* 84, no. 2 (2014): 123–151.

21. McDonald, "Beliefs and behaviors"; Sutlieff, "An absolute prerequisite."

22. Matthew Beckstrom, *Protecting patron privacy* (Santa Barbara, CA: Libraries Unlimited, 2015).

23. Meriam-Webster, "audit," retrieved April 12, 2020. https://www.merriam -webster.com/dictionary/audit

24. San Francisco Public Library, *Privacy policy*, retrieved March 5, 2020. https://sfpl.org/about-us/privacy-policy

SIX

Privacy and Security in the Virtual Library Environment

Hasheed is a library technologies coordinator at a midsize academic library in the upper Midwest United States. Traditionally, his job duties include maintaining library electronic resources and systems (public and employee computers, laptop and iPad rentals, library website, etc.) and working the "Ask Us for Help" desk for 10–15 hours per week. On March 13, 2020, Hasheed received an email from the library's dean announcing the closure of all campus buildings and a transition to online instruction and library services the following Wednesday, March 18. Hasheed would be tasked with working with all library employees to set up web conferencing services for meetings and virtual reference and remote access to library systems and data.

Though Hasheed was responsible for security on library systems, he had no prior experience with remote library services and access. He knew that remote information sharing poses significant unique risks to security, but had a lot to think about in terms of ensuring the safety of both the 50+ library employees and the 10,000+ potential patrons among university employees and students. After gathering information from a variety of sources, Hasheed considered the best way to communicate this information to the service population—a note on the website, a mass email, a post on the university's daily mailing list? There were so many thoughts and concerns, and so little guidance available.

AN EMERGING CHALLENGE IN A TIME OF CRISIS

The 2020 COVID-19 pandemic introduced a paradigm shift to how library services are provided. Many employees, including those who work on the front lines with patrons, made a difficult adjustment to remote work. For some libraries and learning organizations, like universities, remote work may become a greater norm for some positions; regardless, an event like the COVID-19 pandemic informs us of the risk that library employees, at a short notice, may have to shift from traditional to virtual services for an indeterminate length of time. In a situation of great stress, privacy may be an afterthought. However, this logic is tremendously flawed. It is exactly situations like this one on which predators feast. Like in a nature show, the lions swarm the herd of buffalo, increasing their chances of catching a few weak links within the group. Unlike buffalo, if online predators feast on one individual, they are mere steps away from eviscerating the entire herd.

As library and information professionals, one of our primary roles is to ensure that the information shared by patrons does not fall into the hands of unauthorized individuals who might use this information to cause irreparable harm. Predators do not take time off during a crisis—in fact, they do the opposite—so neither should the information professionals responsible for preserving patron privacy. This chapter, utilizing the COVID-19 pandemic as a case study, surveys the practices of information professionals in protecting information privacy while offering remote services and identifies best practices from across the literature of information privacy and security.

What Did Libraries Do?

Libraries took many different paths in responding to the 2020 COVID-19 pandemic. Given that it was a rapidly evolving situation, many libraries introduced one plan early on, only to reverse course a few days later. A study by Wang and Lund looked at how libraries responded in real time.[1] As of March 14, 2020 (three days after the National Basketball Association shut down indefinitely due to the pandemic, seemingly setting off a chain reaction of closings), 68 percent of 80 randomly selected public libraries in the United States had announced a closure, while 86 percent had canceled all library programs. Eighty-two percent of these libraries provided information about remote library resources. Almost all of these announcements/information were provided on the library's website and a social media post, though a few were shared on the website/social media of the municipality the library served (e.g., New York City's government website). Only 26 percent of the announcements were "made" by the library director, with most simply being posted by the website administrator. Certainly, several changes occurred over the course of the next month. By early April, all of the 80 libraries had closed and canceled all services, and all provided information about remote services. However, only a handful of libraries provided information about privacy/

security concerns during the pandemic (including while using remote library services).

Some libraries, particularly academic libraries, are fortunate to be part of an organization that had its own virtual private network, or VPN (Part III of this book has more information about what these are). For instance, Princeton University offered a couple of options for remote access VPNs to its patrons during the COVID-19 pandemic, as did MIT.[2] Of course, not every library, or even every academic library, has the resources of these institutions. Many libraries simply use their library login to restrict access to the library's databases and electronic libraries and utilize email and chat to conduct reference. Zoom may be a possibility, but a secure link is sent to a student if the query is determined to require a zoom session. This appears to be the case with St. Catherine's (MN) university library and many large public libraries like Chicago Public.[3]

Midsize public libraries offered a variety of approaches. Albright Memorial Library (Scranton, PA) simply added a pop-up notice that the library was closed to the public, but any online services were still available.[4] Tompkins County Public Library (Ithaca, NY) offered online library cards for those who did not already have a physical card and broadened access to digital materials.[5] For some small public libraries, the pandemic was a good opportunity to update their website and electronic offerings. Osage City (KS) public library put out a recently remodeled website with a wide variety of services, including genealogy and career services, for its service population of slightly over 3,000—though phone reference was still the primary format of contact with library staff.[6] None of these libraries, however, had any security in place other than regular user authentication.

Many academic libraries, during the 2020 COVID-19 crisis, developed web pages with resources for library users. Many of these resources offer very insightful information about the virus and the library's services, like the University of Washington, the University of Miami, the University of North Carolina, and Middle Tennessee State University.[7] However, no information about online security is provided. Due to the rush to transition to remote services, it appears that privacy has been somewhat overlooked. However, many of the library website policies that existed before the pandemic, as discussed a bit in the prior chapter, suffice for remote access privacy policies. For instance, at the aforementioned University of Miami, they have a website data privacy statement (and quite a nice, detailed one at that) that states what types of information are collected automatically by University of Miami web pages: IP addresses, information about your operating system and browser used, date and time of website visit, pages and links visited, and words searched on the site. It also dictates what can be done with this data: mostly, use it to improve systems and services. All the data is anonymized (names are not collected in any way—unless you search them, I guess). That may not assuage the concern of users, but it is certainly more than just shrugging away the concern about data privacy.

The American Library Association provides some strong privacy guidance that may help improve the policies of many libraries.[8] This includes guidance about library public access computers, as well as a complete COVID-19 resource set called "Pandemic Preparedness Resources for Libraries." Many of these resources simply discuss the response of various organizations and libraries to the pandemic; however, a few resources provide information about library privacy during this time. The Library and Information Technology Association (LITA) offered "A Crash Course in Protecting Library Data While Working from Home"—an extremely relevant e-course to the content of this chapter, and completely free for the public.[9]

How Did Other Departments Respond?

A good object for comparison in this situation is higher education as a whole (as opposed to just the academic library). For instance, the University of Miami has a section on its Information Technology department's pages that includes a diverse selection of policies related to remote access to educational resources.[10] This includes guidance on creating strong passwords, protecting user data, and reporting accidental loss of privacy (such as due to phishing attempts). All of the other academic libraries discussed in this chapter also have some variation of policy offerings on their university or IT websites. Perhaps academic libraries could save themselves a lot of time by simply linking to these policies' web pages? Public libraries could do something similar. The United States' Social Security Administration and Office of Personnel Management both provide detailed guidance on telework/remote access.[11] These resources could be linked from the remote services pages of public libraries.

WHAT DO RESEARCHERS SAY?

Information systems literature has several things to say about the imperative of securing at-home access of organizational information and services. Jorge Chavez recommends that all employees be issued a computer by their employer that is password protected, is designated to be used only by the employee and only for work-related matters, and is connected to a VPN.[12] Anyone exchanging information with an employee (like a patron, in the case of a library) should also utilize a VPN that is provided by the organization. Education should be provided to all of these users about potential Internet scams and security attacks that might occur. Again, the herd is only as strong as its weakest member. While, undoubtedly, not all libraries can afford each of these measures, those that can should employ them. Those that cannot may be able to take other precautions that, while less secure, nonetheless minimize the overall risk of attack. These include storing organizational information and services within a singular system (for a small library, this may be Gmail and Google Drive, which is okay) and ensure that all individuals who have access have secure passwords (not "Library1"). Training about risky behaviors, like opening suspicious emails or responding to queries that ask the employee to divulge any personal information about themselves, is incredibly beneficial. Cybercrime is often seen as a massive battle, but often it is a single individual who manages to dupe an employee into sharing personal information or granting access to private, secure systems.

An increasingly "hot" topic in libraries is data management, including research data management. This is a role that may be maintained by remote librarians, with access through personal computers. This is a particularly messy area of remote operations and security, as a breach in the security of research data compromises both the library and the validity and ethical obligations of the research and researchers. Even library use data and evaluations are data that respondents expect to be held with utmost security, and a breach can irreparably harm trust in the library and university. Hart as well as Culnan, Foxman, and Ray suggest that remote employees who will have access to sensitive data receive training in data security practices, with consistent refreshers to keep it at the top of the employees' minds, and allow the organization's IT staff to manage the install of malware protection and other software to ensure it is done appropriately to provide the greatest security.[13]

Interestingly, some researchers have worked to identify factors that predict the adoption of online information security behaviors. Hazari, Hargrave, and Clenney utilize the theory of planned behavior (a theory quite often used in the study of information behavior, relevant to the understanding of information users, like library patrons, as well) as a framework to study information security behavior of individuals working from home.[14] Knowledge/awareness played an immense role in behavior—knowledge not of computers or the Internet in general, but of information security practices—as did easily accessible information to create that knowledge/awareness (e.g., training modules). Factors like gender, however, played no discernible role, indicating that the information security behavior is not innate but rather learned. This again stresses the importance of regular training for all employees handling or interacting with organizational information.

WHAT CAN LIBRARIES DO?

Certainly, libraries can utilize VPNs and other technologies discussed in Part III of this book. However, these technologies provide no benefit to libraries' employees and patrons unless they are properly educated on how to use them. Thus, offering some training service, before the need for remote services arises, may be advisable. Events like the 2020 COVID-19 pandemic bring new clarity to the need for such training *before* another event occurs. Libraries—and, to be fair, all organizations—were thoroughly unprepared for an event that would negate its purpose as a *place* for engaging with information and community. Unlike in the weeks following an event like 9/11 or Hurricanes Katrina or Sandy, the library could not be a place of shelter or normalcy—unless this function of the library could be transferred to the virtual environment. However, this cannot be truly accomplished unless the virtual environment is secure and private. This includes the offering of virtual programs using videoconferencing technology, which faces threats of hacking that compromises privacy.

A simple measure all libraries, regardless of size, funding, or staff, can take is to provide information on the library's website and social media about information security practices. These include the selection of secure passwords (not "library1"), the use of secure websites (HTTPS, not HTTP), and not sharing personal information on websites/social media. A reminder that times of crisis are also often those in which predators employ their most insidious tactics to exploit security is valuable. Emails offering jobs, like a part-time job as a dog walker, can be enticing for a college student who lost their job or someone just looking to make a few extra bucks. They are also a good excuse for hackers to get unsuspecting applicants to provide personal information including email addresses, phone numbers, legal names, even social security and bank numbers.

As far as email communications during times of remote services/work, it is important to remind all individuals who might receive a message from you to check the address line on an email. Users can edit the name on their "from" line to appear as though they are someone you know (like your supervisor), while the email address would reveal that this is a scammer in disguise. Users should also be informed to always be skeptical of any unsolicited (unexpected) email that asks for them to provide personal information or do something like purchase a gift card for an individual. The best practice if such an email is received is to contact the individual using another contact method that you know is secure (e.g., sending a text message) to confirm the legitimacy of the message. Remember the ABS (always be skeptical). As an example of how all the guidance provided in this

When Online, Always Remember Your ABS:

Always

Be

Skeptical

Phishing attempts abound in the virtual world, and particularly when we feel most vulnerable. Be sure to always question the origin of email and social media messages. If someone asks for personal information or financial help, be sure that you know who they are and that the message is legitimate (for instance, by sending them a text message or direct email).

Figure 6.1   Example of a Social Media Post with Information about Online Privacy

chapter can be synthesized into a visualization suitable for a social media post, take a look at Figure 6.1.

Ultimately, some very small steps may help patrons tremendously. Adding just a short statement to inform patrons about enhanced security risks during a period of remote work/library access, as suggested by the American Library Association, can raise their level of concern and care about these issues. Brief online educational sessions and social media posts like that above can provide guidance that is otherwise difficult to obtain in the chaos of an event like the COVID-19 pandemic.

CONCLUSION

Remote library services pose a serious challenge and burden beyond those already posed in regular library services, as discussed throughout this book. This challenge is only amplified when the need for remote library services is caused by some crisis like the COVID-19 pandemic. At the time of this chapter's writing, virtually all libraries in the United States are closed due to the pandemic, and it is evident, in surveying these libraries' websites, that many lack sufficient resources to promote secure access to library services during this time. This presents additional barriers between patrons and the information they need for health, financial, leisure, and other purposes. This situation is also illuminating, though, in that it highlights areas in which we can continue to improve services to our patron populations following the conclusion of the crisis.

NOTES

1. Ting Wang and Brady Lund, *Announcement information provided by United States' public libraries during the 2020 COVID-19 pandemic*, retrieved February 2, 2020. https://doi.org/10.1080/01616846.2020.1764325

2. Princeton University, *Using library resources from off-campus*, retrieved April 11, 2020. http://web.archive.org/web/20200407225236/https://library.princeton.edu/services/technology/off-campus-access; Massachusetts Institute of Technology, *Virtual private network (VPN)*, retrieved February 7, 2020. http://web.archive.org/web/20200207065339/https://ist.mit.edu/vpn

3. St. Catherine's University, *Services*, retrieved April 12, 2020. http://web.archive.org/web/20200411160056/http://library.stkate.edu/services; Chicago Public Library, *Update on CPL response to coronavirus (COVID-19)*, retrieved April 8, 2020. http://web.archive.org/web/20200408230840/https://www.chipublib.org/news/cpl-response-to-coronavirus/?_ga=2.167359422.1413601037.1584974860-821962295.1584974860

4. Albright Memorial Library, *Home*, retrieved April 8, 2020. http://web.archive.org/web/20200408230258/https://lclshome.org/b/albright-memorial-library

5. Tompkins County Public Library, *Online resources*, retrieved April 5, 2020. http://web.archive.org/web/20200405004025/https://www.tcpl.org

6. Osage City Public Library, *Osage City Public Library*, retrieved April 11, 2020. http://web.archive.org/web/20200411162455/https://osagecitylibrary.org

7. University of Miami, *University of Miami Libraries' remote services*, retrieved April 13, 2020. http://web.archive.org/web/20200413024211/https://www.library.miami.edu/about/remote-services.html; University of North Carolina, *University of North Carolina Libraries' COVID-19 updates*, retrieved April 7, 2020. http://web.archive.org/web/20200408043805/https://library.unc.edu/covid-19-updates/; University of Washington, *University Libraries' remote resources and services*, retrieved April 7, 2020. http://web.archive.org/web/20200407224644/https://www.lib.washington.edu/coronavirus/remote; Middle Tennessee State University, *James E. Walker Library remote services*, retrieved April 13, 2020. http://web.archive.org/web/20200413222912/https://library.mtsu.edu/remote-services

8. American Library Association, *Safety and security in libraries*, retrieved April 15, 2020. https://libguides.ala.org/safety-security

9. Becky Yoose, *A crash course in protecting library data while working from home*, retrieved April 15, 2020. http://www.ala.org/lita/crash-course-protecting-library-data-while-working-home

10. University of Miami, *UM faculty, staff and students policies*, retrieved April 3, 2020. https://www.it.miami.edu/about-umit/policies-and-procedures/index.html

11. United States Office of Personnel Management, *Telework guidance*, retrieved April 3, 2020. https://www.telework.gov/guidance-legislation/telework -guidance/security-it; United States Social Security Administration, *Working remotely: Home office safety and security*, retrieved April 4, 2020. https:// choosework.ssa.gov/blog/2020-01-30-working-remotely-home-office-safety-and -security

12. Jorge D. Chavez, *Key considerations for ensuring the security of organizational data and information in teleworking from home*, retrieved April 11, 2020. https://www.researchgate.net/publication/340389338_Key_considerations _for_ensuring_the_security_of_organisational_data_and_information_in_ teleworking_from_home

13. Mary J. Culnan, Ellen R. Foxman, and Amy W. Ray, "Why IT executives should help employees secure their home computers," *MIS Quarterly Executive* 7, no. 1 (2008): article 6. https://aisel.aisnet.org/misqe/vol7/iss1/6; Jason Hart, "Remote working: Managing the balancing act between network access and data security," *Computer Fraud and Security* 11 (2009): 14–17.

14. Sunil Hazari, William Hargrave, and Beth Clenney, "An empirical investigation of factors influencing information security behavior," *Journal of Information Privacy and Security* 4, no. 4 (2008): 3–20.

PART III

Emerging Technologies: Where Are We Going (and What Should We Do about It)?

A very good question indeed. Our data is worth a lot of money, and people are constantly finding new ways to collect and use it without our knowledge. From social media sites to the content of our email messages, nothing is truly "safe." Yet there are some bastions of hope out there, whether they be simply educating ourselves about trends in data protection or the technologies we elect to use that may help preserve our privacy. Part III of this book discusses some topics in online privacy that have not received much attention in libraries yet—but are guaranteed to enter our collective consciousness within a few years, or less. Here we are presented with the opportunity to be innovators and leaders in the adoption of new privacy measures that will continue to extend the security of our patrons' data.

SEVEN

Tracking Your Web Use

Slipping his library card back into his wallet, Jack Armstrong grinned at the librarian on the other side of the counter. "It's pretty exciting about the upcoming elections, isn't it?" His white teeth gleamed against the dusky hue of his skin as he picked up the short stack of books he had checked out, straightened them, and slipped them into his messenger bag. Chelsea Glover, who had worked at the library for years and knew Jack's conversations could be both long-winded and controversial, raised her eyebrows, creating a new pattern of freckles on her face and forehead. "How so?" she asked, looking idly around the library in hopes of an interruption.

"Come on. Haven't you been reading the news? Everybody is saying the governor had an affair with her husband's brother. Such a scandal, and this is a swing state! We need to be sure not to lose it to those right-wingers with their good old boy networks." Jack was already starting to get fired up, eyes glinting as they flashed first to his right, then his left. "Mark my words, it'll come to no good!"

"Jack, I read the local news online this morning, and saw part of the Early Edition show on TV. Nobody I saw mentioned any such thing. Where have you come to hear about this?"

"It's all over my Facebook page, and my wife Carolyn's, too. I always knew that woman would be trouble, from the day she got elected."

Jack and Carolyn were both in their 70s, and Carolyn in particular was known for her very liberal and frequently vocal stance on political issues. Because neither of them was particularly good using a computer, they tended to come to the library to catch up on their email, read Facebook, and sometimes shop online, even though they had a desktop computer at home. They did so because there was always someone at the library to help them when they got stuck or confused by what was being presented on the screen. More than once, Chelsea had been able to stop them from replying to email that attempted to collect their personal information. Cocking her head to one side, Chelsea asked, "You've only seen this information on Facebook?"

Jack sensed Chelsea's skepticism. "They have links there, to other websites and such. Plus, Carolyn has a friend who said she knows all about it."

Chelsea smiled and nodded, considering her words carefully. "Did you know, Jack, that sometimes people or companies share information that isn't quite true? That you can be tracked and targeted, based on what you've read and what you've looked at on the Internet?"

"No. Why would anybody want to do that?"

"Well, maybe to stir up just the kind of opinion you're already starting to have, for one thing. Or to make you want to buy something. Or, sometimes, people want to convince you to give your information to them."

"Like the guy who called the other day to tell me something was wrong with my computer and he could fix it over the phone? My son said I should hang up on him, so I did."

"That was smart of both you and your son," Chelsea said.

"Maybe Carolyn and I should look a little closer into this whole thing," Jack said reluctantly. "Would you help us get started? Maybe in a few days we could come by."

"Glad to do it, Jack. Tell Carolyn I said hello."

Chelsea thought about the best way she might help Jack and Carolyn, and had to admit the topic was important for more patrons than just those two. She knew how easy it could be for even the savviest social media user to fall for news stories that were unreliable, not entirely correct, or completely untrue. As the idea for a new series of programming in the library started to take shape, she began a mental review of the various ways users' data could be harvested and then information targeted to them, sometimes in very helpful ways, but other times in ways that painted a most untrue picture. She knew that the explosion of social media use, where anyone with an account could claim to be an expert, had resulted in the misinformation and disinformation that might appear seamlessly alongside authentic, accurate news reporting. How could this all have come to pass so quickly?

WHAT DO WE NEED TO KNOW?

Let us go back to examine how we got to the point where web data collection became the big business that it is today. Years ago, most web pages were static, which meant they were designed to be read as a print item might be, but in a new, digital format. The content posted would remain as it was created until someone manually updated them; as a result of this, early web pages were often created to be informational in nature. These pages used HTML (hypertext markup language) exclusively. The Internet Archive is a fun way to see what some of these early sites looked like.

- Here is a 1997 version of our publisher's website: https://web.archive.org/web/19970110002151/http://abc-clio.com/.

- Here is the American Library Association's website, circa 1996 (and my, is it ugly and full of broken links): https://web.archive.org/web/19961029021814/http://www.ala.org/. The "Contact" page did not even include any email addresses!

As technology advanced, the sheer number of website pages requiring updates was coupled with frustration by page creators who wished to influence the appearance of their site pages. Marc Andreesen, a programmer behind the Mosaic browser, wrote on a mailing list, "In fact, it has been a constant source of delight for me over the past year to get to continually tell hordes (literally) of people who want to—strap yourselves in, here it comes—control what their documents look like in ways that would be trivial in TeX, Microsoft Word, and every other common text processing environment: 'Sorry, you're screwed.'"[1] From this, Håkon Lie, in 1994, provided a working document describing the use of cascading HTML style sheets (CSS), "designed so that style sheets can be cascaded; the user/browser specifies initial preferences and hands the remaining influence over to the style sheets referenced in the incoming document. This will provide publishers with stylistic influence without resorting to page description languages."[2]

How does this relate to content sharing and data collection? At the time, it didn't much. It was the next step of website creation, which involved the use of scripting languages, that made pages more responsive and provided information specific to an individual user. The development of Java, JavaScript, PHP, SQL, and the like in the mid-1990s ushered in what became known as Web 2.0, allowing for user interaction rather than the simple display of static text. The correct date and time might be displayed on the page, as an example, or a text field might allow a user to input information, such as an address or other contact information. Dynamic pages use server processing as an aid to locate, store, and return information based on an individual's input, and "the final content of a page is determined only when the visitor requests a page from the web server. Because the final content of the page varies from request to request based on the visitor's actions, this kind of page is called a dynamic page."[3] Here is a 2006 example of the ALA's website, which offers much more dynamic features than its predecessor of 10 years earlier (including log-in and search features): https://web.archive.org/web/20060628232538/http://ala.org/.

Cookies and Privacy

With every technology advance, it seems, comes an offsetting negative effect. In the case of site personalization and the ability to "place mark" your data on various pages, that exchange is the ability for businesses to collect, store, and sell your data, stripping you of your rights to privacy. Such large companies as Equifax, Capital One, and Facebook's famous Cambridge Analytica scandal have affected as many as 330 million users; Yahoo's 2013/14 data breach left no user unscathed, according to the company.[4]

Somewhat similar to the baked treats that share their name, browsers incorporate the use of "cookies," a packet of text information sent to your browser by a web server the first time you visit one of its site pages. Cookies have commonly been used on websites since 1994.[5] Cookies were originally used to improve the user's experience by retaining certain information and improve functionality. As an example, Amazon's site pages tell us, "Cookies are unique identifiers that we transfer to your device to enable our systems to recognize your device and to provide features such as 1-Click purchasing, Recommended for You, personalized advertisements on other Web sites . . . , and storage of items in your Shopping Cart between visits."[6] This is accomplished by your browser adding small text files that collect information when you land on a web page.[7] Cookies have evolved to the point that they're now collecting and storing more and more data about users, as you leave a trail of "cookie crumbs" that will reconnect you to information you've previously seen, saved, etc. on various site pages. Like other items related to the Web, understanding cookies can be more complex than might first seem to be the case, and unfortunately, if you simply use the default settings provided by your browser vendor, you're allowing them to set your privacy standards. This isn't always the best practice, as Dennis O'Reilly notes. "These vendors have their best interests in mind, not yours."[8] It pays, then, to understand what cookies are beneficial, and which might be tracking your private information, and the settings that will improve your privacy and that of your patrons.

Libraries, too, often offer information and language about the cookies their sites use. The Corry, Pennsylvania Public Library offers this message:

> We use browser cookies to ease your access to our catalog and databases. . . .
> These cookies do not collect, store, or maintain your personally identifiable
> information. You do not have to accept these cookies in order to visit or
> use our website and resources, and you can choose to refuse cookies or
> delete cookies from your hard drive. . . . If users choose not to accept the
> cookies generated by such third party database applications, they will not
> be able to use some of those services online; use of the remainder of the
> Library website will not be affected. Be assured that cookies, by

themselves, cannot be used to reveal or discover the identity of the individual user nor are they collected or stored on any library server.[9]

How to Manage Your Cookies

From your desktop, it is possible to view cookie instances in the browser. As of this writing, one simply accesses Firefox > Preferences > Privacy & Security > Manage Data; because the utility is browser-based, these settings are consistent across desktop/laptop devices. For Google Chrome, open and sign in to the browser. Use the three stacked dots at the top right of the interface and choose Settings > Advanced > Privacy and security > Site Settings > Cookies and site data. For Safari, choose Preferences > Privacy >.

To protect yourself from mobile tracking, simply open the Firefox app, choose the stacked bars to bring up the options menu, and choose Settings > Tracking Protection > and choose the level of data that is saved. You can also use the Data Management setting to determine which of your private data is cleared on browser close.

For users of Safari on an iPhone, open Settings > choose Safari > and swipe down to the Privacy and Security Section. As with the Firefox browser, you are also able to clear your history and data from the privacy area.

Mobile Chrome browser users can open the app and click the three horizontal dots to bring up the menu > Privacy. You are able to change settings as needed.

Attack of the Robots

In conjunction with these activities, search engines use small programs called web crawlers to methodically collect, harvest, and save content from web pages.[10] At Google, crawlers "look at webpages, searching for content follow links on those pages, much like you would if you were browsing content on the web. They go from link to link and bring data about those webpages back to Google's servers."[11] Also sometimes called spiders or spiderbots, or web robots, these software applications use scripts to navigate the World Wide Web at a very fast rate, due to their automated, well-organized approach. Their purpose is to store new, previously "unseen" (undetected) links for later indexing, making user searchers more efficient and providing results that are up-to-date.[12]

Phishing

Another gambit often employed by cybercriminals who wish to collect information about you, your location, your various logins, your bank account and social security numbers, and other sensitive information is phishing. In these scenarios, scammers use email, text messaging, or even the telephone to elicit information from you, often using the name of a familiar company or with the tacit or overt threat of something negative happening (your email will be turned off, your account information needs to be updated or you will lose access, etc.). In one recent example, a user's email account delivered a message that purportedly offered a gift card from Walmart. All the user needed to do, the message said, was to click the link, provide a few details, and the gift card would be theirs. Of course, this was an attempt to collect information on the individual, and the sender had no association with the company itself. This type of attempt happens all the time, and the messages can seem to come from the most reliable of sources.

In fact, however, the Crime Complaint Center at the Federal Bureau of Investigation reported that $30 million was lost to phishing activities in one year, and that complaints related to tech support fraud showed losses at nearly $15 million.[13] The Federal Trade Commission (FTC) Consumer Information division notes that as time passes, phishing attempts grow more and more sophisticated and can seem very real to the user who comes across them.[14] One reason for this is social engineering. Social engineering attacks don't exploit technology vulnerabilities; rather, they are aimed at the people who use them. In these scenarios, "phishers" and other scammers attempt to "find a way to deceive a trusted user into revealing information, or trick an unsuspecting mark into providing him with access. When trusted employees are deceived, influenced, or manipulated into revealing sensitive information . . . no technology in the world can protect a business."[15] Businesses are certainly not the only entities at risk, as it is also impossible in all cases to protect the library patron whose intentions are to do well for others, who are curious (and sometimes dream of avarice), or who simply want to look at the next cute picture of kittens and puppies. Their relative innocence is played upon. Schemes to elicit personal information from users is rampant: this writer has culled email after email out of her system asking for business partnerships, extorting for money by saying they've recorded unsavory video of me while on the PC (I run a Mac), and using the gift card ploy that is so common. Although I personally know full well that there is no Nigerian princess or widow who needs me to help her take a few million dollars for safety, the fact is that not all computer users are as savvy. The elderly, those for whom English is not a first language, less educated users, and those who come to the library to access email because they have no other means to do so have neither the experience nor, in some cases, the literacy levels needed to properly interpret these messages and understand them for the scams they represent.

Librarians can help patrons recognize these attempts using the FTC's guidelines and other available documentation to inform training sessions.[16] Even though you might see a corporate logo or name that looks familiar to you, you will often see misspellings, generic address lines, and other telltale signs of phishing. The example in Figure 7.1, which I received via email today, contains many of them (names have been changed).

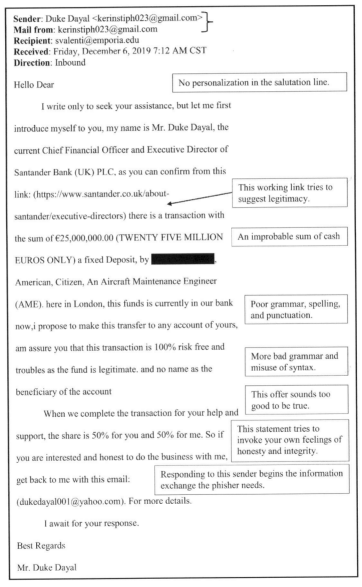

Sender: Duke Dayal <kerinstiph023@gmail.com>
Mail from: kerinstiph023@gmail.com
Recipient: svalenti@emporia.edu
Received: Friday, December 6, 2019 7:12 AM CST
Direction: Inbound

Hello Dear
> No personalization in the salutation line.

I write only to seek your assistance, but let me first introduce myself to you, my name is Mr. Duke Dayal, the current Chief Financial Officer and Executive Director of Santander Bank (UK) PLC, as you can confirm from this link: (https://www.santander.co.uk/about-santander/executive-directors)
> This working link tries to suggest legitimacy.

there is a transaction with the sum of €25,000,000.00 (TWENTY FIVE MILLION EUROS ONLY) a fixed Deposit, by ▮▮▮▮▮▮,
> An improbable sum of cash

American, Citizen, An Aircraft Maintenance Engineer (AME). here in London, this funds is currently in our bank now,i propose to make this transfer to any account of yours,
> Poor grammar, spelling, and punctuation.

am assure you that this transaction is 100% risk free and troubles as the fund is legitimate. and no name as the
> More bad grammar and misuse of syntax.

beneficiary of the account
> This offer sounds too good to be true.

When we complete the transaction for your help and support, the share is 50% for you and 50% for me. So if you are interested and honest to do the business with me,
> This statement tries to invoke your own feelings of honesty and integrity.

get back to me with this email:
> Responding to this sender begins the information exchange the phisher needs.

(dukedayal001@yahoo.com). For more details.

I await for your response.

Best Regards

Mr. Duke Dayal

Figure 7.1   Example of a Phishing Email

A common case that academic librarians may face is the spam journal email. These emails solicit submission of manuscripts to a supposed "peer reviewed journal." Often the email portrays the journal as being revered, having a high impact factor. The journal's name may be very similar to that of a prestigious journal in the author's discipline (e.g., the *Journal of Information Science and Technology* instead of the *Journal of the Association for Information Science and Technology*). These journals do not have peer review (though they may pretend they do) and charge inordinate sums of money for publication. One of the authors of this book reported a total of over 100 of these spam emails over a period of just three months in early 2020.

A review of several best-practices lists from around the web offers these tips for identifying phishing attempts:

- Legitimate companies with whom you have an account will usually call you by name;

- Poor spelling and grammar are suspicious, especially from major businesses, who frequently hire professional copywriters;[17]

- It's important to remember that companies that are legitimate won't ask for your sensitive information over email. They understand the risks that are involved.[18]

- Check the name of the person sending the email, but also the email address, by hovering the mouse over the "from" line of the email. Do they match? If not, be doubly suspicious;

- Be very wary of any links that are included in text or emails. Instead, teach patrons to directly type the company's website URL, or to call companies when they have any question about a link's authenticity;

- Watch out for offers of business partnerships, money stewardship, lost relatives, and so on, where the writer asks you to respond with your personal information, and remember the adage "if it seems too good to be true, it probably is";

- Most of all, be very vigilant when considering how and whether you will respond to email. No antivirus software can help when someone voluntarily shares their private information with a hacker or cybercriminal.

To support librarians' efforts, the FTC offers a "Just for You: Librarians" resource page from its Consumer Information division, at https://www.consumer.ftc.gov/features/librarians. To increase the ability for patrons (and library staffs) to understand how to recognize phishing attempts, the FTC offers "materials in Spanish, videos, presentation slides with talking points, some worksheets and lesson plans" to help with program development and delivery for topics on what to do about identity theft, how to recognize a charity scam, and more.[19] They provide free bookmarks, infographics intended to be branded with your library's information (this is public domain content), and free print publications. One additional feature of these site pages is their focus on specific patron groups: military families, patrons who are incarcerated or reentering the community, kids and teens, and the elderly population.

Ransomware and Malware Attacks

The Cyber + Infrastructure division of the Department of Homeland Security (CISA) defines ransomware as "a type of malicious software, or malware, designed to deny access to a computer system or data until a ransom is paid. Ransomware typically spreads through phishing emails or by unknowingly visiting an infected website."[20] A certain amount of money is demanded once the malware has been installed from the user, whether an individual or organization. In a library setting, this might mean loss of catalog access and other data; for users, it could mean a complete lack of access to their personal devices. However, ransomware attackers can also use social engineering techniques. My spam folder recently contained a message of which Figure 7.2 is a part.

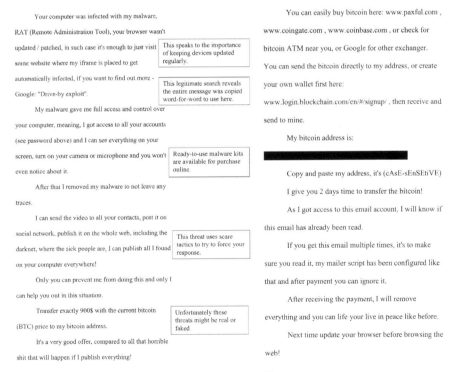

Figure 7.2   Example of a Ransomware Email

It's obvious that this might seem to be a real threat for some (this type of campaign is also known as a sextortion email scam[21]); however, in this case I knew the ransomware threat was not valid for several reasons, not the least of which is my innocence with regard to the charge made by the ransomer. Today, Trojan horses, programs that were created with the express purpose of breaching a computer's security when the user believes another function is running, represent an ongoing threat. "Computer viruses are a real nightmare for any Internet user. Among them, the so-called Trojan Horses are the most commonly encountered and some of the most malicious."[22] But, as with other phishing schemes, the "human factor" in the phishing world, $900 might not seem like a high price to pay for a user to regain their privacy. Members of our society might well fear the delivery of such explicit content to others, and depending on a person's situation in life, it might seem appealing to pay this sum of money for the problem to go away. The problem with ransomware payments is that there is no guarantee that your data or access will be returned to you, that your machine won't be affected again in the future, or that the ransomer won't attempt to extort more money.

Password Protection

One first protection for many of the personal details you share via the web is the use of a strong password. Librarians, when working with patrons, are frequently tasked with helping out with account setup, including password selection and recovery, and in this capacity can also offer help and advice as to how to create strong passwords rather than weak ones. While programs are used by cybercriminals to help guess your passwords, the passwords users create often offer the only barrier available to protect their data. The CISA recommends these actions:[23]

- Use of multi-factor authentication. When it is available, as is common in banking and other financial accounts, the two-factor authentication process combines your password with another means of authentication: a retinal scan, a text code, or your finger, face, or voiceprint.

- Use different passwords for different systems and accounts. This is especially important, as using few passwords is like giving someone a master key. Several accounts could be hacked at once.

- Don't use passwords that are based on personal information that can be easily accessed or guessed. So your name, or your street, or the name of your favorite cat or dog are all out. Additionally, we've all heard the joke about the 1-2-3-4-5 password, and apparently there is truth in the humor: SplashData, a security company, recently released its eighth annual list of worst passwords of the year. Culled from 5 million passwords that were leaked on the Internet, these are the top five:[24]

1. 123456

2. password

3. 123456789

4. 12345678

5. 12345

- Based on the information above, it's smart to use the longest password or passphrase permissible by each password system. Often pass phrases are now being suggested: an example might include four words chosen at random: sink-crash-spinner-farm is estimated by one algorithm to take about 93 centuries to attack, while the password 12345 takes 0 milliseconds.[25]

- Consider "salting" the password with symbols and numbers to make it harder to detect. The famous phrase "to be or not to be" when parsed as tobeornottobe lists an approximate crack time of nine minutes using the algorithm above; changing it to ?2Bornot2B! lists a crack time of one century; the phrase to-be-or-not-to-be lists a time of 134 centuries, and is much easier to recall.

- Don't use words that can be found in the dictionary, regardless of the language. As with other passwords, dictionary terms alone are easier to crack.

- Refer to the CISA's Tips on Choosing and Protecting Passwords[26] and Supplementing Passwords[27] websites for more information

Two free resources can help inform this process as you get started. Both were created and are managed by Microsoft's Troy Hunt, who says he does so "as a free resource for anyone to quickly assess if they may have been put at risk due to an online account of theirs having been compromised or 'pwned' in a data breach."[28] This site is called ';—have i been pwned? After accessing https://haveibeenpwned.com, a user simply enters an account name to see if the account has been subject to a data breach. If the account or site has been compromised, you know it's time to change passwords associated with it. Hunt's other project is similar, seeking out passwords that have previously been hacked. Similarly to the account pwned site, one simply navigates the browser to https://haveibeenpwned.com/passwords and enters a password that is current in use or one that one might wish to use. Hunt, on his site pages, notes, "I wanted to keep it dead simple to use and entirely free so that it could be of maximum benefit to the community."[29] This utility has identified more than a half million passwords that were previously exposed in data breaches.

Because they have been exposed in the past, these passwords should not be used, as they're at much higher risk of being used to take over other accounts.

HOW TO APPROACH WEB TRACKING POLICY: WHAT LIBRARIES SAY

All right, so all this knowledge is well and good, but how do we apply it to develop good library policy? Let us look at how a few libraries have approached developing policy around web tracking and cyberattacks.

King County (Seattle, WA) Public Library contracts with BiblioCommons to host its web services.[30] BiblioCommons has a clear section on the site (under "Privacy Policy") that lists what types of information are collected from users of the site:

- Personal information, including library barcode information, name, birth month and year, and email address. This information is used to create a user account and monitor your activity.

- Borrowing information: What resources have been borrowed/accessed from the library's systems

- Shared content: information such as rating and reviews of books and lists of books "to read" or "recommended"

- Feedback and suggestions: Any comments submitted to the library (these are not considered confidential)

- "Non-identifying information":
  o Browser type or IP address to help determine how the site is used by users
  o Search log data ("anonymized")
  o Google Analytics
  o Other account data (anonymized and displayed only in the aggregate)

- The site also describes how this information is safely stored and under what circumstances it can be accessed by others (such as the police).

- Additionally, the website does state that it uses cookies to "improve user experience." The website actually provides a clear and succinct description of what cookies are: "cookies are small files used to enhance the functionality of websites or to record browsing activity." So at least there is no lack of clarity about what cookies are or whether they are being collected on the site.

Furthermore, the site does include a statement on data tracking on other websites: "The Internet is a big place: Take care to guard your personally identifying information. This website may link to other websites that collect personal information. We recommend that you review the privacy policies of these sites before providing them with any personal data."[31]

The New York Public Library similarly (and, perhaps, unsurprisingly) has a strong online data collection policy statement.[32] It provides a list of information that is collected by its website, along with definitions to clarify. It discusses how and why this information is collected, and it explains the significance of cookies. Perhaps most importantly, it provides contact information (both an email and a phone number) that individuals can contact if they have any concerns or want to remove any information.

The King County Library and New York Public Library sites check nearly all of the boxes you would want them to in addressing data collection on the site. While elements of the policy (like the collection of cookies) may be points of debate, the fact that the site clearly states its policy at least allows users to make informed decisions about using the site. Like with a health waiver for skydiving or whitewater rafting, you know the risks. Comparatively, many library sites provide very little detail. Looking at the sites of other public library systems in or near the Seattle metropolitan area, many have no statement to address these privacy concerns, or a very short one.

One problem with creating this policy—which we allude to in the introduction to this section of the book—is that the topic is fairly complex. Library directors are not expected to be experts in online data collection and may not even know what data their systems are collecting and what is being done with it. This is really a topic that a systems analyst would be more capable of addressing. Of course, most libraries (particularly small and rural ones) do not employ system analysts, and these analysts—where they do exist—may not understand the enhanced need for privacy within libraries. Many small libraries use a third-party service, like WordPress or Wix, for creating their site. In these cases, employing a consultant to help with drafting a policy may be worthwhile (a few companies, like ProQuest, offer system consulting services on a sliding pay scale). In the absence of these solutions, libraries may at least say 'we don't know, so proceed at your own risk,' or, as one library's website states, "The Internet is not a secure medium."

One element of the King County Public Library's website that is particularly beneficial is the statement about external sties. While we may not worry too much that our library is going to do something nefarious with our patrons' data, we cannot be so sure with other sites. The Library of Congress may have the most detailed version of this warning.[33] They provide links to the privacy policies of every external site to which their site links, including social media, vendors, event services, surveys, videoconferencing, and downloadable software. Additionally, the site describes the types of online information that is commonly collected by websites and why (e.g., cookies).[34]

As for phishing, ransomware, and other cyberattacks, few libraries offer direct guidance in this area, instead considering it part of "general computer knowledge" for which libraries are not responsible. But perhaps they should be, especially when these threats can directly harm the libraries themselves if they occur on a public library computer. Traditionally, warnings by libraries about these types of cyber threats occur only after-the-fact. Education about phishing attacks is not provided until one occurs and the library finds it prudent to inform patrons about the threat. One example is a post by Syracuse University Libraries in 2019, which warns of a phishing email that asks students to follow a link in order to reset their library username and password.[35] Another case was reported in December 2020 involving Glen Ellyn Public Library in Illinois, where a caller allegedly posed as library staff in order to solicit individuals' personal information.[36] The University of California (Berkeley) has an example of a phishing email directed at library users that walks through each element that should raise users' concern.[37]

Often, universities rely on their IT departments to educate students, faculty, and staff about these threats. The University of Michigan, University of Virginia, and Rochester Institute of Technology are all among the universities that rely on IT to inform the campus population of phishing and other threats.[38] These sites, to their credit, provide very good information. For instance, Rochester Institute's site describes what phishing is, common types of phishing attacks, how to identify a phishing attack, and examples of real phishing attacks used against the university. The University of Michigan provides a web page that lists all of the existing phishing threats on campus, allowing the campus community to easily check whether the email they have received matches a known threat (of course, that could backfire if the threat is new and not yet posted on the site). This approach to educating the public is all well and good, but academic libraries should still have their own plan to educate the public as well as they deal directly in the area of information seeking and use and may be more visible to many students on campus.

That is fine for academic libraries, but what about public libraries? What role could they be playing in educating their patrons about online security threats? This is an area where few public libraries really have a plan—but some do. Mid-Continent Public Library (serving suburban Kansas City, Missouri) has a detailed web page with information about spam and phishing, including screenshots that walk patrons through the process of identifying these messages.[39] The Boston Public Library shared a blog post in 2020 that describes what phishing is in celebration of National Security Awareness Month.[40] During the COVID-19 pandemic, San Francisco Public Library offered virtual education sessions on cybersecurity topics including spam, phishing, and malware threats.[41] These excellent approaches should be considered by more public libraries as yet another way to support their communities.

WHAT RESEARCHERS SAY

Researchers tend to be a bit more philosophically focused on the ideal than the practical, and evidence of that fact will be clear in this and the following two chapters. The guidance offered by these researchers, nonetheless, provides an important perspective on what the privacy-minded and information rich–minded researcher might have to say about libraries participating in web tracking.

One thing to note in the "positives" column for web tracking is that it is essentially an automated way to evaluate patrons' information behavior.[42] Based on information that may be readily collected from library websites, you can piece together how patrons interact with library systems, what searches they use, and what types of information resources they prefer (historically, transaction log analysis has been a popular research method that employs this approach).[43] This information can, in turn, inform the maintenance and redesign of these systems. That is, in essence, the purpose of all this collection of information in the first place. Libraries are in the business of gathering, maintaining, and using information. On the surface, it all makes perfect sense that libraries would want to collect and use patron information.

However, many researchers and ethical philosophers appear to raise alarm at the idea of collecting any user data other than that which is absolutely vital to the library's service functions. There are, evidently, at least two reasons why researchers/philosophers might favor barring any collection of non-vital data:

1. The library cannot completely ensure that the data collected will not be accessed by third parties. Whether it is a false sense of security in using third-party applications on the library's website or insecure ways of storing the data the library collects itself, there is no certainty to ever offer.

2. It is not your data to collect. Sure, we would all like to know as much about other people as possible. It would help us to predict their behavior—which is, of course, beneficial in manifold ways. In libraries, we would love to know more about patrons in order to improve their experiences. It is one thing if people volunteer this information in order to help you, and another if you sneakily collect it without them really knowing what is going on.[44]

In fact, we know that when people are made aware of data collection risks, they often make efforts to avoid it. This is why there is a whole burgeoning industry for web browsers that automatically block the collection of user data: browsers like Brave and Tor (which we discuss in Chapter 9). Researchers like

Pan, Cao, and Chen have proposed algorithmic solutions that validate the source of data requests from websites to prevent unwanted tracking.[45] Libraries should be aware of these developments—even if they plan to keep collecting user information on their sites—because it is likely that more patrons will begin to request access to these browsers as security threats become more apparent to the average user.

There are common features of spam email and phishing attempts that can be central to distinguishing these messages from valid ones. They often include a large number of grammatical errors and use language (especially greetings) that do not seem quite right. If you read the messages with an uncritical eye, you are likely to write off these elements as typing errors or minor language differences—and they might be!—but if you read with a critical eye, you will know to at least be a bit more skeptical of these elements (like when evaluating information resources in general).[46]

Significant amounts of research in IT/systems discuss approaches to phishing education that may be integrated by librarians into their instruction (yes, we know there is already a lot on your plate, but this one is important!). Robila and Ragucci, for example, provide seven steps to developing a phishing education program:

1. Learn what phishing is
2. Understand the implications of phishing
3. Discuss the ways phishing can be detected
4. Discuss the ways phishing information can be collected
5. Discuss ways to evaluate phishing education
6. Fill out phishing IQ (pre-/post-test)
7. Discuss general results and evaluate the session.[47]

Really, this design is quite similar to the one-shot library instruction that is offered at many universities—just replace "phishing" with "misinformation" or "fake news." Many instructional librarians are used to teaching in this way, and integrating security concepts into this type of an instructional session would not cause dramatic reimaging of the instructional process.

WHAT WE SAY

Have a clear and informative policy in place. Describe what web tracking is and what types of information your site collects and why. Disclose the fact that you cannot guarantee that external sites that patrons visit will be as secure or ethical with patrons' data as you are. We do not want to make a judgment on whether a library *should* collect users' data—there seem to be both positives and negative to doing so—but we do recommend that your decision be communicated clearly to patrons.

As for cyberattacks, we recommend that you look at some of the excellent examples we reference for academic and public libraries. There is a significant role for libraries in educating the public about information security topics like these ones. Similar to information literacy, security literacy is a domain that relies on educating the public about "common sense" cues that elucidate the veracity of information. Distinguishing a phishing email from a valid email is not too dissimilar from distinguishing "fake news" from legitimate news. Security literacy education can be an important extension of the information literacy instruction that we already offer.

CONCLUSION

This chapter dived into the back end of our library systems to investigate how our policies for online information collection, retention, and use can impact our patrons. While there is disagreement as to the extent to which this information should or should not be collected, it seems clear that patrons should be informed about its collection. There are reasonable risks that many people will take in exchange for something they want (like improved user experience on a website), but they should not be left in the dark about these risks. Hopefully, this chapter has provided guidance on what information libraries should include in their privacy policies to keep patrons aware.

NOTES

1. Bert Bos, *A brief history of CSS until 2016*, Colophon, retrieved November 13, 2019. https://www.w3.org/Style/CSS20/history.html

2. Håkon W. Lie, *Cascading HTML style sheets–A proposal*, retrieved September 14, 2019. https://www.w3.org/People/howcome/p/cascade.html

3. Adobe Dreamweaver, *Understand web applications*, retrieved November 11, 2019. https://helpx.adobe.com/dreamweaver/using/web-applications.html

4. Verizon Media, *Yahoo provides notice to additional users affected by previously disclosed 2013 data theft*, retrieved October 24, 2019. https://www.verizonmedia.com/press/yahoo-provides-notice-to-additional-users-affected-by-previously

5. Oksana Kulyk, Annika Hilt, Nina Gerber, and Melanie Volkamer, *"This website uses cookies": Users' perceptions and reactions to the cookie disclaimer.* (Paper presented at the European Workshop of Usable Security, London, England, April 23, 2018.) https://dx.doi.org/10.14722/eurousec.2018.23012

6. Amazon, *Amazon.com privacy notice*, retrieved January 1, 2020. https://www.amazon.com/gp/help/customer/display.html/ref=help_search_1-3?ie=UTF8&nodeId=201909010&qid=1567632788&sr=1-3

7. Oksana, *"This website uses cookies."*

8. Dennis O'Reilly, *Three not so simple but necessary security tips*, C|Net, retrieved December 3, 2020. https://www.cnet.com/how-to/three-not-so-simple-but-necessary-security-tips

9. Correy Public Library, *Privacy policy*, retrieved November 21, 2019. http://corrylibrary.org/about-the-library/library-policies/privacy-policy

10. Sebastian Thrun, *Web Crawler: CS101, Udacity*, retrieved November 21, 2019. https://www.youtube.com/watch?v=CDXOcvUNBaA

11. Google Search, *How Search organizes information*, retrieved November 5, 2019. https://www.google.com/search/howsearchworks/crawling-indexing/

12. Computer Science Wiki, *Web crawler functions*, updated November 14, 2019. https://computersciencewiki.org/index.php/Web_crawler_functions

13. Federal Bureau of Investigation, *2017 Internet Crime Report* (2019). https://www.ic3.gov/media/annualreport/2017_IC3Report.pdf

14. Federal Trade Commission Consumer Information, *How to recognize and avoid phishing scams*, updated May 2019. https://www.consumer.ftc.gov/articles/how-recognize-and-avoid-phishing-scams

15. Kevin D. Mitnick and William L. Simon, *The art of deception: Controlling the human element of security* (Indianapolis, IN: Wiley Publishing, 2003), 3.

16. Federal Trade Commission, *Just for you: Librarians*, retrieved November 5, 2019. https://www.consumer.ftc.gov/features/librarians#Gettingstarted

17. Rick Broida, *How to spot a phishing email*, C|Net, retrieved November 24, 2019. https://www.cnet.com/how-to/spot-a-phishing-email

18. David Ellis, *7 ways to recognize a phishing email: Email phishing examples*, retrieved November 7, 2019. https://www.securitymetrics.com/blog/7-ways-recognize-phishing-email

19. FTC, *Just for you: Librarians.*

20. CISA, *Ransomware guidance and resources*, retrieved October 15, 2019. https://www.us-cert.gov/Ransomware

21. Christine Howler, *Trojan: Drive by exploit email*, retrieved March 8, 2020. https://howtoremove.guide/remove-drive-by-exploit-email

22. Ibid.

23. CISA, *Creating and managing strong passwords*, retrieved March 8, 2020. https://www.us-cert.gov/ncas/current-activity/2018/03/27/Creating-and-Managing-Strong-Passwords

24. John Hall, *SplashData's top 100 worst passwords of 2018*, TeamsID, retrieved December 13, 2018. https://www.teamsid.com/splashdatas-top-100-worst-passwords-of-2018

25. *Why should I use a random passphrase?* Use a Passphrase, retrieved November 14, 2019. https://www.useapassphrase.com

26. CISA, *Security tip (ST04-002): Choosing and protecting passwords*, updated November 18, 2019. https://www.us-cert.gov/ncas/tips/ST04-002

27. CISA, *Security tip (ST05-012): Supplementing passwords*, updated January 21, 2020. https://www.us-cert.gov/ncas/tips/ST05-012

28. Troy Hunt, *Who, what, & why*, retrieved February 9, 2020. https://haveibeenpwned.com/About

29. Ibid.

30. King County Library System, *BiblioCommons U.S. privacy statement*, retrieved December 27, 2020. https://kcls.bibliocommons.com/info/privacy

31. Ibid.

32. New York Public Library, *Privacy policy*, retrieved December 13, 2020. https://www.nypl.org/help/about-nypl/legal-notices/privacy-policy

33. Library of Congress, *Third party websites, services, and applications commonly used by the Library of Congress*, retrieved December 19, 2020. https://loc.gov/legal/third-party-websites-services-and-applications

34. Library of Congress, *Website user and online collections privacy policy*, retrieved December 19, 2020. https://loc.gov/legal/privacy-policy

35. Syracuse University Libraries, *Alert: Libraries phishing email circulating*, retrieved August 1, 2019. https://libnews.syr.edu/alert-libraries-phishing-email-circulating

36. Lisa Marie Farver, *Scam alert: Glen Ellyn Library warns of phishing attempts*, retrieved December 1, 2020. https://patch.com/illinois/glenellyn/scam-alert-glen-ellyn-library-warns-phishing-attempts

37. University of California-Berkeley, *Phishing example: Library account*, retrieved December 29, 2020. https://security.berkeley.edu/news/phishing-example-library-account-0

38. University of Michigan, *Phishes & scams*, retrieved December 30, 2020. https://safecomputing.umich.edu/phishing-alerts; University of Virginia, *Examples of phishing and scam emails*, retrieved December 30, 2020. https://security.virginia.edu/examples-phishing; Rochester Institute of Technology, *Phishing*, retrieved December 30, 2020. https://rit.edu/security/content/phishing

39. Mid-Continent Public Library, *What is phishing?*, retrieved December 29, 2020. https://mymcpl.org/blogs/what-phishing

40. Boston Public Library, *Cybersecurity and cybercrime*, retrieved November 5, 2020. https://bpl.org/blogs/post/cybersecurity-and-cybercrime

41. San Francisco Public Library, *Technology: Tech Tuesday—Don't get phished*, retrieved December 21, 2020. https://sfpl.org/events/2020/07/07/technology-tech-tuesday-dont-get-phished

42. Ina Fourie and Theo Bothma, "Information seeking: An overview of web tracking and the criteria for tracking software," *Aslib Proceedings* 59, no. 3 (2007): 264–284.

43. Michael Hooper, "Tracking visits to a library website using Google Analytics," *Tennessee Libraries* 59, no. 3 (2009). https://search.proquest.com /docview/1559896572/fulltext/CE3BB8EFD2DD4B1FPQ/1?accountid=27180; Amy Vecchione, Deana Brown, Elizabeth Allen, and Amanda Baschnagel, "Tracking user behavior with Google Analytics events on an academic library website," *Journal of Web Librarianship* 10, no. 3 (2016): 161–175.

44. Steven Englehardt, Dillon Reisman, Christian Eubank, Peter Zimmerman, Jonathan Mayer, Arvind Narayanan, and Edward Felten, "Cookies that give you away: The surveillance implications of web tracking," *Proceedings of the International Conference on the World Wide Web* 24 (2015): 289–299; Tatiana Ermakova, Benedict Bender, Benjamin Fabian, and Kerstin Klimek, "Web tracking: A literature review on the state of research," *Proceedings of the Hawaii International Conference on System Science* 51 (2018): 4732–4741.

45. Xiang Pan, Yinzhi Cao, and Yan Chen, "I do not know what you visited last summer: Protecting users from third-party web tracking," *Proceedings of the Annual Network and Distributed System Security Symposium* (2015). https://doi .org/10.14722/ndss.2015.23163

46. Brady Lund and Ting Wang, "This is NOT spam: An analysis of predatory publication invitations in library and information science," *Proceedings of the ASIST Conference* 57 (2020): e344.

47. Stefan Robila and James Ragucci, "Don't be a phish: Steps in user education," *ACM Sigcse Bulletin* 38, no. 3 (2006): 237–241.

EIGHT

How Public Computer Network Usage May Pose a Threat

USING THE PUBLIC INTERNET

"Pull over soon, could you please, Dexter? I need to use the facilities."

Dexter rolled his eyes but scanned for the next exit sign on the Interstate. "Again? Ok. We're coming to another town just up ahead."

"Works for me!" Reaching over, Henry gave his partner a light punch in the shoulder. "I don't want to sound like a nine-year-old, but how long until we get there?"

"You should stay awake and watch, and then you'd know." It was all foolishness, of course. Friends since grade school, they both knew Henry couldn't stay awake in a moving car for more than a few miles before he was sawing logs. It had fallen then, to Dexter, to drive to the state's public library conference for their presentation on early literacy.

"Come on, you know I try to stay awake."

"Try harder!" Then Dexter relented. "It's a good hour to the state line, and then another 90 minutes or so until we get to the conference hotel."

Pulling into town, Dexter saw a large national coffee shop directly off the Interstate. The words "Public Wi-Fi!" were colorfully emblazoned in the window. "How about here? Facilities and caffeine."

"As long as there's a restroom. Hey, while I take care of business and get us something to snack on, why don't you see if you can download the next book in that series we've been listening to?"

"Sure. I've got the hotspot we checked out from the library. There are a couple of documents I need to send over to my branch director, too."

"Great. You don't mind if we stay a few minutes, do you? I'm going to grab my laptop so I can check our presentation one more time, and I'll want to catch up on my email before we get back on the road."

"That sounds like a plan. I could use a little bit of time away from this steering wheel! Just don't forget to use the library's VPN client to keep your data safe."

Henry's eyes widened. "Oh, yes! Thanks for the reminder."

CONSIDERATIONS WHEN USING OPEN PUBLIC NETWORKS

When considering the issue of open public networks, think about the last time you were at the coffee shop, or a fast-food place, or maybe at the airport. You might be inclined to simply tap one of the networks your phone or other device displays as being available. Many coffee shops and other retail outlets offer this kind of free, open-access Wi-Fi for anyone who is in or near their building. This is often also true in the case of libraries, whose networks can offer havens of access to Internet resources. According to the Federal Trade Commission, though, "Wi-Fi hotspots in coffee shops, libraries, airports, hotels, universities, and other public places are convenient, but often they're not secure. If you connect to a Wi-Fi network and send information through websites or mobile apps, it might be accessed by someone else."[1]

In these cases, it can be impossible to know whether other users on (or creators of) the network you see displayed on your device represent hackers or scammers attempting to scrape your passwords, data, and other information while you're connected. It can also, at times, be difficult to be certain that the network you access is actually bona fide; after all, anyone could create an open network—what if "7–11," "seven eleven," and "7 11 Guest" all appear on your list of available networks? One way to be sure you've selected the right network is simply to "verify the name of the network with staff or on signage before connecting"[2] to help ensure your safe access.

A good way for anyone to protect their privacy on open networks is to ensure you only visit websites that you know have been encrypted. "Encryption scrambles the information you send over the internet into a code so it's not accessible to others."[3] To determine whether a website has encryption protocols in place, simply look at the address bar of your browser. If you see http://awebsite.com, you can know it is not encrypted. A website using the URL https://awebsite.com does use encryption protocols, so is safe. The difference is the "s" following the http. That changes the acronym from *hypertext* *transfer* *protocol* to *hypertext* *transfer* *protocol* *secure*. Remember, though, that these are websites, not the wireless hotspot network point itself. "Hackers can easily take control of a Wi-Fi router, even official ones, if they are not properly configured."[4]

As you log onto a public website, think about your reason for access. If you need to provide credit card information, check on your bank accounts, or conduct other potentially high-risk transactions, you will be safer using a private network in your home, or employing the use of a virtual private network, where available, to protect your data. You might also consider such browser add-ons as Force-TLS and HTTPS-Everywhere, which are free for Firefox and "force the browser to use encryptions on popular websites that usually aren't encrypted."[5] Librarians should let patrons know, though, that these add-ons do not work for all websites, and they should be sure to check for "https" in the URL line of any website accessed.

VIRTUAL PUBLIC NETWORKS (VPN)

Before beginning a discussion of VPNs, it's important to understand the purpose and use of your computer's internet protocol (IP) address. You might wonder if you even have one, and the answer is yes if your computer, phone, tablet, and so on is connected to the internet. Much like your home address, your computer's IP address tells other computers where your network "lives" on the web and geographically, in order to deliver you your data, including your mail, search results, and so on.[6] The website whatismyipaddress.com will display your current IP address, as well as the city and state in which you're located, for those who are interested.

VPNs use encryption to hide your IP address and location. In the process, your plain text is scrambled into a new, unreadable format called cipher text.[7] Your VPN service takes that scrambled data and "puts your internet data into a capsule, of sorts, to send it through a private tunnel to the website you requested."[8] T. J. McCue, senior contributor to *Forbes*, reminds us that although a VPN can provide safe user access to various types of content, using the private browsing feature of a browser isn't enough: "Many people think that the 'private browser' tab on Google Chrome or Firefox will shield all of their activity. It will not."[9]

Having IP address information exposed to others can be risky, especially when conducting transactions where security is important, such as when passing sensitive information about the library over the Internet. Patrons checking out hotspots and laptops need to know about the risks of using these devices, especially over a public network, as discussed earlier.

Library organizations can offer training to patrons and staff for VPN services. VPN services can be offered for staff only, or for broader use. During the COVID-19 outbreak, Princeton University Library's web pages advise that all faculty staff and students working off campus utilize their Secure Remote Access system, a "Virtual Private Network (VPN) service managed by Princeton's Office of Information Technology."[10] A quick Google search on April 17, 2020, revealed that the University of California, the University of Arkansas, Yale, and the University of Florida, among other academic libraries, recommend using VPN services when accessing content from off campus.

Another time a VPN might be of value is when traveling internationally. As one international VPN vendor notes, "Accessing websites from abroad can be difficult without the use of a Global VPN client. Country specific websites block content to visitors trying to access them from foreign countries."[11]

Using a VPN can provide another level of privacy and security in day-to-day computing, whether on the laptop or desktop, or a mobile device. Libraries, too, can make VPN access available on their networks. But why should they do so?

In May 2018, the U.S. House voted to kill the Federal Communications Commission's (FCC) regulations regarding the use or sale of user data collected by Internet service providers (ISPs).[12] What that means is that Comcast, Verizon, AT&T, and others can use content they access based on your browsing history, purchases, and so on to make recommendations for products and services. The FCC had, the previous October, created two tiers of privacy sensitivity: These data categories are no longer protected by the FCC's privacy regulations:

- Geographic location
- Children's information
- Health information
- Financial information
- Social Security numbers
- Web browsing history
- App usage history
- The content of communications
- Your name
- Your address
- Your IP addresses

- Your current subscription levels
- Anything else not in the "opt in" bucket.[13]

These kinds of risk for data breaches impel all of us act to protect our privacy, don't they? Unfortunately, according to a 2018 survey conducted by *PC Magazine*,[14] the answer is no; in fact, in 71 percent of 1,000 survey responses collected over the period of February 7–9, 2018, participants reported having never used a VPN at all.[15] Results of another study, conducted by Patricia Norberg and her colleagues, confirm the idea people give more private information than they at first agree they will, calling this the "privacy paradox."[16] Their study was conducted in two phases among a sample of part-time graduate students. In the first, participants were asked to fill out a paper-and-pencil questionnaire to measure activity as it was related to behavioral intention. A series of checkboxes described various personal information items that might be requested by a bank, which would pay a $20 incentive for providing it. This included such personal information as name, number of credit cards, loans, addresses, family income, online shopping preferences, and so on. Twelve weeks later, in the second step of the study, a mock "banker" came in the room to inform students of a program it was piloting, targeted toward graduate college students. Each individual was asked to complete a coupon book, which asked for the same personal information as earlier. No monetary incentive was given. Participants were told to leave blank any items they felt uncomfortable sharing, and the booklets were collected to analyze the data. Results showed that of the 55 participants who attended both phase one and phase two of the study, "the level of actual disclosure significantly exceeded individuals' intentions to disclose."[17] In light of these findings, the need for more digital literacy instruction at the library level is clearly indicated, as well as the provision of VPN services to protect the personal information and identity data of the patrons and staff who use their networks. As libraries select and maintain their integrated library systems, the ALA recommends that modern encryption services, with up-to-date security protocols, be used, and that where client applications do not support this encryption, should use VPN technologies.[18] Similarly, in the K–12 environment, the ALA notes, "Client applications that do not support encryption (such as staff desktop clients) should employ virtual private network (VPN) technologies. In addition, any personally identifiable information and student data housed by the library or school off-site (cloud-based infrastructure, tape backups, etc.) should use encrypted storage.[19]

Who offers the best VPN service? An open Google search using the string "best VPN 2019" reveals several site hits. Among them are results from

C|Net, PC Magazine, Forbes, PC World, and *MacWorld*. Pricing is included on some of the site pages, and *PC Magazine* offers a nice comparison table so that individuals can choose a plan based on its options and pricing, along with a review for each.[20]

LIBRARY PUBLIC ACCESS COMPUTERS

"The bedrock foundation for intellectual freedom," as noted by the ALA, "is the right to privacy."[21] In order to support libraries as they work to uphold patron intellectual freedom, the ALA offers several privacy checklists surrounding the topic. Of particular interest to this discussion is the checklist regarding public access computers.[22] The checklist of action items is based on priority of need, to offer a practical series of steps toward improved patron security. The ALA determines priority-one-level actions to include issues directly impacting each user:

- Using print signs or computer home screens to give information about Wi-Fi privacy and library policy, after the library first determines its threshold for risk and sets policy surrounding privacy levels versus conveniences offered

- Using a software such as Deep Freeze coupled with browser privacy settings to purge downloads, browsing histories, and room reservations on logout and destroying paper sign-up sheets for all devices after use

- Provide technology training and other materials regarding computing best practices, as well as privacy screens for patrons who request them[23]

At the next priority level, library systems are addressed. This includes the installation and use of antivirus software, anonymizing and destroying patron records after use, configuration of content filters—so data is not stored, anonymizing and destruction transaction/network logs after use, and the need to conduct regular security audits.[24]

Various security installations themselves comprise the set of priority-three actions. The checklist itself notes that priority levels two and three might be harder to implement, depending on how skilled library staff are, current systems in place, and resource availability for purchase and installation. The ALA recommends the use of HTTPS Everywhere, Privacy Badger, guides regarding browser security options, the installation of the Tor browser, Tails OS or the like (which forces incoming and outgoing connections to go through Tor), as well as network segmentation into subnets, use of malware blockers and antivirus programs, and ensuring that data is not automatically shared with software publishers, such as error reporting logs.[25]

The ALA Privacy web page also encourages that "a proactive process should be created to notify ongoing users of any changes to the library's privacy policies."[26] This additional step will help ensure that patrons are kept current with the many changes occurring with technology as the library implements them. The New York Public Library website offers these caveats, as an example, regarding public wireless access:

- The Library's wireless network is not secure. Information sent from or to your laptop can be captured by anyone else with a wireless device and the appropriate software, within three hundred feet.

- Library staff is not able to provide technical assistance and no guarantee can be provided that you will be able to make a wireless connection.

- The Library assumes no responsibility for the safety of equipment or for laptop configurations, security, or data files resulting from connection to the Library's network.[27]

SHARING YOUR PHOTOS AND IMAGES ON THE WEB

Did you know that others are able to track you via photographs you have taken? Just as with each book, database article, or other item contained in the library's collection, images contain metadata that can provide additional information about them. The date and time of the image, the camera's exposure settings, even the altitude at which the image was taken can be determined. The image's size, compression type, and color settings are stored. Additionally, global positioning system (GPS) can pinpoint the physical location of the person at the time the photograph was taken. This occurs based on the use of exchangeable image file format (Exif) data.[28]

As with other types of technology, Exif data offers the opportunity to benefit users or put them at risk, depending on how it's stored and shared. To the user's benefit, Exif data can help people sort their images by date or location. The metadata allows both users of the library and its marketing and archival staff to create digital repositories of events, people, and memories, and then locate them via date or keyword search.

Considering the amount of information available here, it easy to see why it could be useful for someone (a web designer or photographer) to glean this type of information, but it can also cause privacy concerns for someone who considers themselves vulnerable.

GOOGLE TRACKING

Even when you feel you've taken the proper precautions with your site use, have implemented strong passwords (see Chapter 7, and changed your social media and browser settings to protect your privacy, you may not have done enough. Did you know that Google continues to track their users' geographic locations, even after they've opted out of/turned off tracking? Associated Press investigator Ryan Nakashima reports, "Google wants to know where you go so badly that it records your movements even when you explicitly tell it not to" after discovering that Google stores your location information even after you've changed your privacy setting to prevent them from doing so.[29] Like so many technologies, the tracking feature in Google can be beneficial or worrisome. For example, parents may wish to know their children's whereabouts, or that of a spouse or other family member. On the other hand, an ex-spouse or other individual who feels at risk might not wish to be tracked. Vacationers, especially, might want to have their locations set to private so others aren't aware of their absence from their homes. Google Tracker allows PC and Android users to do this; Mac and iPhone users can implement use of the built-in tracker that makes that possible.

PCMag contributors Chandra Steele and Jason Cohen offer detailed information on how your privacy settings can be manipulated using both Mac- and PC-based platforms.[30] Accessing myaccount.google.com will allow you to update not only your personal information, but your data, security, sharing, and payment options, and which third-party accounts have permission to share your data.

During a discussion of patron technology issues in the public library, one of the writer's students commented that it was common for patrons to ask them what their password was when they needed help with email or other accounts. Many others chimed in immediately about the importance of librarians not only to be knowledgeable about the systems and platforms they used themselves for work and pleasure, but also to know the particulars of others. Issues of age, socioeconomic status, English-language capability, level of education, and various levels of cognitive and physical abilities all have an impact on today's library user. The "vast majority of people in the world probably have good intentions, but it is the small number of individuals with psychopathic tendencies or those who are simply willing to do things that most others would find immoral that create the need for proper security around one's personal data."[31] I, for one, can't overstate the importance and value of those front-line librarians who do so much, in so many ways, to help protect the privacy of our patrons' data and digital footprints.

HOW LIBRARIES HAVE USED THESE CONCEPTS TO INFORM POLICY

VPNs are one area where the difference between academic and public libraries (and large versus small academic libraries) is quite pronounced. Many large academic libraries have worked with university IT, or among their own staff, to provide access to a VPN and clearly outline a VPN policy. A few examples from around the United States:

- The University of California Berkeley has a web page (https://lib.berkeley .edu/using-the-libraries/vpn) where they provide a download link for a free VPN to use when accessing library resources. Also included are directions on how to install the VPN and what to expect while using it, as well as contact information if users have any questions. There is also a link to a frequently asked questions page that addresses questions like "How do I start up (the) VPN?" and "Does the VPN work on mobile devices?"

- The University of Illinois's VPN pages—while not quite as clear as Cal's page—contain all the information needed to install and operate their VPN. The main problem is that it does require navigation to multiple pages in order to gather all of the information a novice user would need. The main library information page on the VPN (https://library.illinois.edu/library-technology /vpn/) just includes a few sentences about how a VPN allows users to securely connect to library databases and a link to installation instructions. This link leads to a page (https://help.uillinois.edu/TDClient/42/UIUC/Requests /ServiceDet?ID=167) with another one-line description of what a VPN is and a link to yet another page (https://techservices.illinois.edu/services/virtual -private-networking-vpn/download-and-set-up-the-vpn-client) that actually contains the detailed instructions and download link. So everything is there on the library's website, but it could be better organized for user navigation.

- The University of California Riverside (https://library.ucr.edu/using-the -library/technology-equipment/connect-from-off-campus) provides a series of engaging videos that discuss the basics of connecting remotely to the library's services using the university's VPN. They even have separate videos for Macs, Windows, and Chromebooks. This is in addition to a written introduction and instructions (including screenshots) that are provided on a separate information page. The university's VPN pages are really an exemplar of how all the pieces can fit together from describing what a VPN is, to how to install it, and outlining the rules for its use. If we were to have one complaint, it would be the gnarly-looking URLs for the pages that might make site navigation more difficult (e.g., https://ucrsupport.service-now.com /ucr_portal/?id=kb_article&sys_id=8a264d791b5f0c149c0b844fdd4bcb34).

- Beyond these examples from large academic libraries, mention of VPNs is sparse. In fact, we could really only find two examples of VPNs being mentioned on a public library's website as of this writing:

  o The Seattle Public Library mentions them in regard to the use of the mobile hotspots they lend to patrons.

  o The Brooklyn Public Library has offered a few educational courses on the topic of VPNs in recent years.

The cost of purchasing a subscription to a VPN for all library users is not feasible for most libraries, and free VPNs come with the concern of lack of centralized control (knowing who the users are and being able to provide support). Lack of knowledge of VPNs among the ranks of librarians is likely an underlying factor as well. In this case, let us look at how such guidance could be offered if these libraries did take the opportunity to implement one.

You might want to start by including a statement about what a VPN is, following in line with what the large academic libraries have done. The most successful examples of these statements explain VPNs in detailed, but nontechnical, form. For instance, you might say something like:

- "We highly encourage the use of a virtual private network (VPN) when accessing library resources on a public network. A VPN encrypts and funnels data that is sent over a network in order to ensure privacy and security. It is like an underground tunnel that connects you with the sites to which you want to connect. Connecting to a VPN does not require any knowledge of computer programming or technical details of computers. To install a VPN on your computer, simply follow the instructions on the VPN site. Here are a few VPNs that we recommend. Please note that several of these VPNs do require a paid subscription, though there are several free ones listed as well:
  - Subscription-based VPNs:
    - NordVPN: Perhaps the most well-known VPN, with very good speed, privacy, and security
    - Private Internet Access: Very fast speed and good security, fewer users than NordVPN
    - UltraVPN: Good speed and security, offers a six-month free trial
  - Free VPNs:
    - TurboVPN: Offers both free and subscription options. Free option is slower.
    - Proton VPN: Slower and a bit less secure than subscription-based options."

This fairly simple statement covers all the necessary bases for informing patrons about VPNs, from describing what it is and its value to patrons, to providing suggestions for both subscription-based and free VPN options.

LIBRARY PUBLIC ACCESS COMPUTERS AND WEB TRACKING

As noted earlier in this book, many libraries have a generic privacy policy that warns patrons of dangers of the web—something like "Beware! The Internet is not a secure medium. Use at your own risk!" But those statements are not particularly helpful; they just read like a liability statement that you would sign before going white water rafting. Here, let us take a look at what elements we would recommend to include, based on the information in this chapter and the few existing policy examples that do exist.

Texas A&M libraries does a nice job outlining data elements that are collected from their websites, and this could simply be expanded to warn users about the typical risks they will face on all websites. They note that the information that may be collected directly from users when using websites includes:

- User/client hostname or IP address
- "User-agent" information, such as information about the browser, browser version, and the operating system used
- "Referrer" information, the page that directed the user to the library's page
- System date (of data request)
- Details of the request being made
- Status returned for request
- Size of content returned (in bytes)
- Method of request
- Universal Resource Identifier (URI) of the resource retrieved
- Protocol used[32]

Additionally, the site mentions cookies (including describing what they are) and information about server sessions.

Information about Google Analytics is also provided on the Texas A&M site. The site lists all the types of information that Google may access, which are . . . A LOT.

- IP address
- "User-agent" information
- URI information
- Information about screen color, resolution, etc.
- Mobile device information
- Bandwidth information
- Java and flash information
- Geographic data
- Amount of time spent on a web page

This information all poses a major potential threat. That cannot really be helped from the perspective of the librarian. The point is that disclosure is made of the risks posed on the Internet, as opposed to the traditional "at your own risk" statement.

Wicomico (MD) Public Library similarly has a detailed third-party data information and policy section, though it does not mention VPN use.[33] The site notes, for instance, that third-party services that link from the library site can collect data including: Name, address, library information, IP address, data and time of site use, searches conducted, and pages accessed. The site notes that cookies can be collected on any site (including the library's website). It also provides information about social media use. This is all in addition to traditional privacy, records privacy, and photography policy. This all makes Wicomico's privacy page one of the easiest to read and to find and navigate. It is a great example of how a relatively small public library can inform its users about privacy threats.

CONCLUSION

While web data is often collected by sites—including library sites—in order to help improve user experience rather than for some malicious purpose, informing patrons about the privacy risks associated with this data is nonetheless imperative. VPNs and related privacy-promoting platforms (like the dark web, discussed in the next chapter) can support the needs of patrons with privacy concerns, but only if they know the specific risks they face, what VPNs do to help, and how VPNs can be installed and used. While many libraries lack any information or policy in this regard, a few good examples, from libraries like Texas A&M and Wicomico Public Library, show us how this information can be provided.

NOTES

1. Federal Trade Commission Consumer Information, *Tips for using public Wi-Fi networks*, updated March 2014. https://www.consumer.ftc.gov/articles /0014-tips-using-public-wi-fi-networks

2. Lexy Savvides, *Staying safe on public Wi-Fi*, ClNet, updated June 3, 2015. https://www.cnet.com/how-to/tips-to-stay-safe-on-public-wi-fi

3. FTC, *Tips for using public Wi-Fi.*

4. T. J. McCue, "5 steps to protect yourself on free public WiFi," *Forbes* (June 28, 2019). https://www.forbes.com/sites/tjmccue/2019/06/28/from-airports-to-the -library-5-steps-to-protect-yourself-on-free-public-wifi/#1228e8242a02

5. FTC, *Tips for using public Wi-Fi.*

6. *Without IP addresses, the internet would disappear,*" What Is My IP Address, retrieved April 16, 2020. https://whatismyipaddress.com/ip-address

7. Alison Grace Johnson, *What is encryption and how does it protect your data? NortonLifeLock,* retrieved April 16, 2020. https://us.norton.com/internetsecurity-privacy-what-is-encryption.html

8. T. J. McCue, "How does a VPN work?," *Forbes* (June 20, 2019). https://www.forbes.com/sites/tjmccue/2019/06/20/how-does-a-vpn-work/#15a1b3e870cd

9. Ibid.

10. Princeton University Library, *Using library resources from off-campus,* retrieved April 17, 2020. https://library.princeton.edu/services/technology/off-campus-access

11. VyprVPN, *Access blocked websites globally,* retrieved November 15, 2019. https://www.vyprvpn.com/global-vpn

12. Chris Morran, "House votes to allow internet service providers to sell, share your personal information." *Consumer Reports* (May 4, 2018). https://www.consumerreports.org/consumerist/house-votes-to-allow-internet-service-providers-to-sell-share-your-personal-information

13. Ibid.

14. Max Eddy, "You're not using a VPN? Bad idea," *PC Magazine* (May 3, 2018). https://www.pcmag.com/news/360805/youre-not-using-a-vpn-bad-idea

15. Eddy, "You're not using a VPN?," para. 1.

16. Patricia A. Norberg, Daniel R. Horne, and David A. Horne, "The privacy paradox: Personal information disclosure intentions versus behaviors," *Journal of Consumer Affairs* 41, no. 1 (Summer 2007): 100–126.

17. Ibid.

18. American Library Association, *Library privacy guidelines for library management systems,* updated January 26, 2020. http://www.ala.org/advocacy/privacy/guidelines/library-management-systems

19. American Library Association, *Library privacy guidelines for students in K-12 schools,* retrieved April 2, 2016. http://www.ala.org/advocacy/privacy/guidelines/students

20. Max Eddy, "The best VPN Services for 2019," *PC Magazine* (November 13, 2019). https://www.pcmag.com/roundup/296955/the-best-vpn-services

21. American Library Association, *Privacy,* updated April 2017. http://www.ala.org/advocacy/privacy

22. American Library Association, *Library privacy checklist for public access computers and networks,* updated January 26, 2020. http://www.ala.org/advocacy/privacy/checklists/public-access-computer

23. Ibid.

24. Ibid.

25. Ibid.

26. Ibid.

27. New York Public Library, *Wireless internet access (Wi-Fi)*, retrieved April 17, 2020. https://www.nypl.org/help/computers-internet-and-wireless-access/wireless-internet-access

28. Thomas Germain, "How a photo's hidden 'Exif' data exposes your personal information," *Consumer Reports* (December 6, 2019). https://www.consumerreports.org/privacy/what-can-you-tell-from-photo-exif-data

29. Ryan Nakashima, "AP exclusive: Google tracks your movements, like it or not, *Associated Press News* (August 13, 2018). https://apnews.com/828aefab64d4411bac257a07c1af0ecb/AP-Exclusive:-Google-tracks-your-movements,-like-it-or-not

30. Chandra Steele and Jason Cohen, "How to get Google to quit tracking you," *PCMag*, updated February 11, 2020. https://www.pcmag.com/how-to/how-to-get-google-to-quit-tracking-you

31. Kyle Torpey, "If you don't care about online privacy, you should read this," *Forbes* (February 28, 2019). https://www.forbes.com/sites/ktorpey/2019/02/28/if-you-dont-care-about-online-privacy-you-should-read-this/#1e7127e23886

32. Texas A&M University Libraries, *Website compliance and privacy*, retrieved January 7, 2021. https://library.tamu.edu/about/compliance.html

33. Wicomico Public Library, *Privacy policy*, retrieved January 7, 2021. https://wicomicolibraries.org/privacy-policy

NINE

Letting Your Library Get Stuck in the Dark Web

Preparing for this evening's library training session, Dakota was headed to the printer to pick up a few short handouts for participants. A patron stood near one of the empty public access computer terminals, looking vaguely uneasy and unsure about his surroundings.

Recognizing a chance to meet the patron and offer help with his information needs, Dakota looked over and smiled at the man, who glanced to his left and right before making eye contact.

"Hi, can I help you get started with something?" Dakota approached the man cautiously, not wanting to add to his discomfort. Although the weather wasn't particularly warm that day, the man seemed to be sweating, uncomfortably hot.

Worried eyes looked Dakota up, then down, then back up again. "I don't know. I am trying to find my family back in my home country. I want to let them know I'm okay."

Despite Dakota's caution, one eyebrow winged up in interest and compassion. The man's accent was thick, and his discomfort continued to be plainly visible. Considering options for this patron, Dakota decided this might be a good time to open a Tor web browser to aid in the search on the deep web.

Why Tor? Why the deep web? Good questions, thought Dakota, trying to decide how to explain the concept to the man.

"Let's just try this," Dakota said, reaching around the man to double-click a desktop icon for the Tor browser, and the two worked together for some time.

The man, Dakota later told his colleague, had not yet found his family members, from whom he had been separated when they escaped his home country. He did, however, now know how to best protect his private searching from unwanted eyes.

After his shift, Dakota headed over to the nearby coffee shop for a cinnamon macchiato, a real guilty pleasure. He saw Hinata Tanaka, a newer librarian in his district, already sitting at a table.

"Mind some company?" Dakota asked.

"That'd be great," said Hinata. "I felt like getting a little booster—she pointed to her fragrant tea—and wanted to take a bit of time to enjoy it."

As they talked shop, the conversation eventually turned to Dakota's exchange with the man who had been looking for his family, along with his recommendation that they place Tor browser links as a desktop icon on each of the public use computer stations to allow easy patron access to the dark web.

"Hey, wait a minute." Hinata pursed her lips. "Why would you want that? Isn't the dark web just a place for illegal drug trafficking, and thieves, and the like? Doesn't that mean more risk than reward?" She saw Dakota's automatic head shake and was glad they had a little time so she could learn more.

Dakota offered, "Let's start out with the different types of web access that exist. There are mainly three." Hinata nodded, her eyes urging more information. Following her lead, Dakota offered this explanation.

YOUR DIGITAL FOOTPRINT

By the time the United States moved past World War II and into an unprecedented era of economic growth, the days of the horse and carriage had already passed into relatively distant memory. Automobiles, airplanes, and other motorized modes of transportation had made crossing the country—or the ocean—little more an event than crossing the street. Shopping centers' numbers grew from only 8 at the end of World War II to 3,940 in 1960, and the number of television sets in the United States grew from fewer than 17,000 in 1946 to being purchased at the rate of 250,000 per month three years later, with 75 percent of U.S. households reporting ownership of at least one television by 1960.[1] The Internet's first prototype, the Advanced Research Projects Agency Network (ARPANET), was created in the late 1960s. The first mobile telephone call was made on the streets of New York City, from Martin Cooper to the head of research at Bell Labs on April 3, 1973; its main purpose was to gloat ("Joel, I'm calling you from a cellular phone, a real cellular phone, a handheld, portable, real cellular phone").[2] Importantly, the Transmission Control Protocol and Internet Protocol (TCP/IP) communications model still in use today saw its beginning in the 1970s, and was adopted by ARPANET on January 1, 1983.[3] Regardless of these strides, mobile technology was still in its infancy; on January 8, 1982, Ma Bell was mandated to split its company along regional lines down into the Baby Bells due to the antitrust lawsuit filed by MCI.[4] When Tim Berners-Lee invented the World Wide Web in 1989, things were much different from a societal perspective, and cell phones as we know them today were still a thing of the future: Simon, IBM's "personal communicator," the first device to employ telephony, email, calculator, address book, and on-screen keyboard feature (it could even send and receive faxes!) was not introduced until 1994.[5]

Heraclitus of Ephesus, c. 500 BCE, is known for his assertion that "Everything changes and nothing remains still . . . and . . . you cannot step twice into the same stream" as translated by Seneca,[6] or "the only constant is change" as we know the phrase today. The world of technology has, in recent years, seen that same stream become an ever-raging river, straining against the banks of decency, regulation, morality, and creation. Television set ownership in the United States is estimated at approximately 120 million. Smartphone ownership, as of data collected in fall 2016, was estimated at 84 percent of the population, with one-third of households owning three or more devices.[7] "Taken together, 90% of U.S. households contain at least one of these devices (smartphone, desktop/laptop computer, tablet or streaming media device), with the typical (median) American household containing five of them."[8]

Next up, to add to this electronic overhead? The Internet of Things (IoT). The online *Oxford English Dictionary* defines the IoT as, "development of the internet in which many everyday objects are embedded with microchips giving them network connectivity, allowing them to send and receive data."[9] This includes such obvious technologies as home voice controllers from Google, as well as Amazon Echo or Alexa; doorbell surveillance systems by Ring, Amazon, and others. They can also include otherwise innocent-seeming items such as room/house thermostats, smoke detectors, light switches, and your toaster and coffeepot. Your car might well be connected to the Internet, and your fitness system. Your Apple watch or your Fitbit, along with other wearable technologies, might be purchased, as can robotic vacuums and networked bathroom appliances. Your television today is more than likely a "smart" model, which means it directly accesses the Internet, and your activity can be monitored and recorded there, as well.

Using each of these types of technology today requires some proactive involvement. "Retreating to one's home, closing an office door, or hanging up a phone may have previously allowed a person to feel a measure of control over who might be listening or watching, but the presence of network-connected devices in private spaces can remove this sense of control and privacy."[10] Although the easiest path of action is to take no action at all, taking a hands-off approach to device security is naïve at best, and can be dangerous at worst.

The American Library Association (ALA) is clear on its privacy stance. Their position states that without regard to technology types employed in the library setting, all staff who collect or personally access information that identifies a patron, format notwithstanding, have a legal and ethical obligation to protect patrons' confidentiality. Library technology security practice and policy to safeguard patron information needs to be current and comply with state and national standards. The ALA points to the *National Information Standards Organization* "Consensus Principles on Users' Digital Privacy in Library, Publisher, and Software-Provider Systems,"[11] which requires that practices include:

> encryption of personal data while they are at-rest and in-motion; prompt updates of systems and software to address vulnerabilities; systems, proce-dures, and policies for access control of sensitive data; a procedure for security training for those with access to data; and documented procedures for breach reporting, incident response, and system, software, and network security configuration and auditing.[12]

In order to understand the privacy implications in lay terms for each type of device, this chapter will undertake to provide definition of and background for the various types of web access available to users. Some are obvious, and some not as readily apparent, such as the need for the protections that librar-ies can afford their patrons via the dark web.

Misunderstanding exists about what different parts of the web represent. A recent open Google search of the phrase "what is the dark web" returned some frequently asked questions, such as: Is it illegal to be on the dark web? What is the dark web used for? How much of the Internet is the dark web? How dangerous is the dark web? Can you buy body parts on the dark web? Can you get to the dark web from a phone?

DIFFERENT PARTS OF THE WEB

The Surface Web

This is the Internet you know and have become most familiar with. You might have heard it referred to as the visible web, the indexed web, or the clear web. Other terms are used as well, but this is the part of the web that the common user is most familiar with.

This part of the Internet seems huge, because it is. Here, you find shopping sites, such as Amazon or Wayfair, and more recently grocery store sites that allow you to order online for delivery or pickup. Recipe and cooking sites abound, as do restaurant pages and food delivery companies. You can read magazines online, check out e-books. Or you can get the news. You can do the crossword puzzle or play games, either by yourself or with friends or strangers. You can build islands and other artifacts on Second Life, although that is not so common these days. Facebook, Instagram, and other social media and text/chat service apps are out there in boatloads. You can use online maps to find and explore places, look at images, go to school, watch a movie, or binge a TV series. It's this kind of open content that Google, Bing, Yahoo!, and other search engines navigate to let you know where to get a good pizza nearby, or to listen to your favorite music.

HTTP versus HTTPS

Most of us know today to seek out the HTTPS (Hypertext Transfer Protocol Secure) indication of a secure site for online payments and other financial transactions, but site browser engineers are doing more to offer information about unsecure sites. In Firefox, a user may access an information icon to the left of the address field to determine the site's status.

The current version of the Chrome browser offers a similar feature that is more direct: the menu bar in Chrome gives the flat statement: Not secure. As with the Firefox browser, one may click the information button to learn more and change settings.

Mac users will see slightly different messages: In Firefox, a padlock with a red diagonal shows the site is unsecure; for Chrome, the message appears exactly as on a PC. Mac users who use the Safari browser will see the "not secure" message directly in the address bar.

Libraries use both face-to-face interaction and the Internet to give information access and share resources, and tools are readily available for purchase online that allow eavesdropping and data interception. Marshall Breeding, on the topic, notes that, "Only with strong encryption technologies can information transmitted across networks be considered private."[13] Hypertext Transfer Protocol (HTTP) does not protect the user, and allows for data vulnerability to site impersonators, manipulators, and interceptors.

HTTPS protocols, on the other hand, provide better information security and user confidentiality. Google describes three key layers of protection:

1. Encryption—encrypting the exchanged data to keep it secure from eavesdroppers. That means that while the user is browsing a website, nobody can "listen" to their conversations, track their activities across multiple pages, or steal their information.

2. Data integrity—data cannot be modified or corrupted during transfer, intentionally or otherwise, without being detected.

3. Authentication—proves that your users communicate with the intended website. It protects against man-in-the-middle attacks and builds user trust, which translates into other business benefits.[14]

HTTPS protocols use digital security certificates, which can range in price from no cost at all to upwards of $400, depending on the type of certificate and extent of required validation.[15] The website Let's Encrypt (https://letsencrypt.org) offers free, automated, and open certificate authority.[16] Breeding offers these certificate types:

Extended validation: The certificate confirms the organization's exclusive right to use the domain and performs an extensive review of the organization details relative to official business records. Sites with this type of certificate will present the name of the organization in the URL bar of most browsers along with the indicator that the site is encrypted using HTTPS.

Organization validated: The certificate authority confirms the organization's right to use the domain. If properly validated, the organization's name will be shown when the user views the details of the certificate in the browser. For sites with this type of certificate, the URL bar of the browser indicates that the site is encrypted using HTTPS.

Domain validated: The certificate authority confirms the organization's right to use the domain but does not require extensive documentation regarding the organization. For sites with this type of certificate, the URL bar of the browser indicates that the site is encrypted using HTTPS.[17]

Unfortunately, barriers exist for perfect HTTPS compliance within the library environment. Consider the third-party vendors with which libraries do business, and to whose websites libraries connect. If those sites are not HTTPS compliant, the content must be considered vulnerable. This can be compounded when the library exists as part of another entity, such as a county, city, or educational institution. July 2018 has generally been seen as the deadline for compliance with HTTPS protocols, although Breeding notes that as of October 2019, a "substantial portion remain not in compliance with this essential requirement.[18]

The Deep Web

While some believe the deep web and dark web to be interchangeable terms, there are differences. It is this portion of the web, also known as the invisible web or the hidden web, that houses content not indexed by search engines (more on this to come). Much of this content is related to users' personal records and transactions. The deep web contains such resources as the fee-based database content on the library's servers, individual companies' intranets and extranets, your online banking records, your private email, your health and social security information, information you store in the cloud, and so forth. The content exists behind passwords and sometimes paywalls (based on subscription to a service, like a newspaper or Netflix). Think of the implications if some of these resources could be obtained via an open web search! Dictionary.com (2019) defines the deep web as "the portion of the Internet that is hidden from conventional search engines, as by encryption; the aggregate of unindexed websites, private databases and other unlinked content on the deep web."[19] The deep web, according to INFOSEC, a company whose goal is teaching company staffs how to defend their organizations against cybercrime, offers an estimate of the size of the deep web versus the surface web.[20] The surface web, the sites we commonly see when browsing the web, comprise about 10–16 percent of all websites. The deep web, sites that are hidden behind some kind of barrier such as a log-in page, comprises the remainder. Of the deep web, some unknown, smaller portion is part of the dark web, which requires specialized software in order to access.

If you think about this, it makes sense. After all, virtually everyone has at least one email account, most people go to the doctor, and the government keeps records on all of us, one way or another. Many in the population maintain banking and other financial accounts. Governments and businesses want to (and in many cases, must) keep information private, away from visible web searches. Add in the account information that lives behind your Amazon, Macy's, and other online service providers' firewalls, and it becomes easy to see not only why there continues to be exponential growth of the deep web, but how it got to be so large at all. Here is just one small example: Internet Live Stats, as of 6:31 p.m. CDT on April 16, 2021, showed 628,798,341 Twitter tweets had been made so far *that day*, and at 6:32 p.m., the number was 629,364,321,[21] which represents a rate of 565,980 tweets for that one minute of one day using one particular app.

The Dark Web

There is a small portion of the deep web that is known as the dark web. It is this part of the web to which drug trafficking, child pornography, and other nefarious activities have been ascribed. However, I would posit here that as with any sort of tool, the dark web can be used to benefit users as well as being a place for other types of activity.

Also called darknets, or Darknet, the dark web describes the portion of the deep web that, from a purely technical perspective, Robert Gehl describes as "websites built with standard web technologies (HTML, CSS, server-side scripting languages, hosting software) that can be viewed with a standard Web browser, such as Firefox or Chrome, which is routed through special routing software packages."[22] Those special software packages use protocols that "are undetectable from search engines and offer users complete anonymity while surfing the web. At the same time, Dark Web website publishers are also anonymous thanks to special encryptions provided by the protocol."[23] It is this two-way anonymity that makes the dark web an appealing place for those who wish to remain anonymous.

The dark web was initially created by the U.S. government.

Mariana's Web

A myth? The truth? Mariana's Web is purportedly named after the deepest part of the ocean, Mariana's Trench, and is "supposedly the deepest part of the web, a forbidden place of mysterious evil—or at least, that's the mythos a subset of online believers has cultivated."[24] A search using one university's discovery layer returned only two results for the keyword search "Mariana's Web"; of these, one result was for a newspaper article that discussed dark web content without specifically referencing Mariana's web; the other was a "Field Guide to Virtual Warfare,"[25] published by a group called Adbusters, whose Manifesto site page tells us, "We build the first internet-based global grassroots power bloc in history—a superpower without borders."[26] The Field Guide (which somewhat unsurprisingly carries no author byline) describes Mariana's Web:

> This is the black hole of the Internet. Google it and you'll be told it's a hoax and that it doesn't exist, which in many ways is completely accurate characterization. Mariana's Web is not so much a place you can find . . . you're likely aware that the NSA and its partners have been operating a global surveillance apparatus to spy on American citizens, foreign nationals, various political leaders and pretty much anybody they can bug, tap or hack. But what you may not realize is that these recent revelations are just another chapter in a long, protracted struggle for the control of cryptography.

ACCESSING THE DARK WEB

At this point, you might think that the dark web is only a place where terrible things happen by and mostly to terrible people. However, there is good reason for accessing and using dark web resources. Oppressed people in other countries, as an example, can explore Facebook and the United Nations using the dark web, protecting their anonymity and privacy.[27] Journalists may need anonymity as they try to keep documents confidential; both the journalists and those they interview also may need to maintain confidentiality.[28] Musicians and other artists may wish to avoid censorship of other types.[29] The dark web can help maintain communication channels for anyone where free speech doesn't exist, as in countries where governments eavesdrop on citizens or Internet access itself is deemed a critical activity, and for corporations to protect sensitive documentation.[30] It is the anonymity of the dark web that some find useful or needed. As stated earlier, though, one cannot simply access the dark web using a standard installation of Chrome, or Firefox, or Safari. Instead, a special circuit of encrypted connection is created, using relays on the network.[31]

The implications of anonymity of users' locations, identities, and on occasion, intentions serve other purposes, as well. It important to realize that the dark web is frequently documented as a place where "any number of illegal or immoral transactions are taking place, such as the sale of drugs, prostitution and human trafficking, illegal pornography, and other unsavory activities"[32] The very protections enjoyed by those whose work is private, or somewhat embarrassing, or might put them at risk with their governments are leveraged by more nefarious site visitors who have very different goals. These protections lead law enforcement officials to note that "there are a number of investigative challenges when looking at Darknet markets."[33] Some users employ such tools as the random pathways generated by browsers like Tor and encryption services such as a virtual private network (VPN—more on this later), as well as identifying themselves on the web with frequently changing pseudonyms. In this way, illegal and immoral activities become ephemeral, constantly shifting targets.

Another important draw for all users of the dark web is its relative ease of use. While built using technically advanced program structures, installation and continued access are relatively simple.[34] How-to guides, YouTube videos and other instructional content, and community discussion forums couple with easy to find and use downloads and user-friendly interfaces, eliminating the need for technical expertise or particular depth of knowledge when getting started.[35]

The Onion Router (Tor)

Although not the first, Tor is arguably the most famous dark web browser today. It works by "distributing your transactions over several places on the Internet, so no single point can link you to your destination."[36] Tor was originally developed by the military, but is now open-source software operated by supporters around the world.[37] Tor developers liken the process of searching via their browser to using a twisting, turning path to elude followers—and wiping out your footsteps occasionally as you go along. Because a random pathway uses many relays rather than a direct link from source to destination, each individual relay only knows where that one relay before it originated and where that one relay after it was headed.[38]

To get started using Tor, download and install the application from the website. There is also a version of Tor for mobile for users with Android devices. It uses a proxy app, Orbot, for private mobile browsing.[39] Once you download the file, you can set up your Tor instance using documentation provided for free on its website. Once there, the site defaults to the DuckDuckGo search engine.

I2P

I2P uses the analogy of garlic, as opposed to Tor's onion, where multiple messages are connected—bundled together in a bulb.[40] Unlike other networks that work to make user locations anonymous, I2P doesn't hide the originator or recipient of communicating computers. Instead, I2P was created to allow peers using this browser functionality to "speak" with each other anonymously, which makes each party unidentifiable by the other, as well as to third parties.[41] I2P offers websites within the I2P environment, to allow for anonymous web publishing or hosting; it can also proxy via HTTP to the normal web, in order to create an anonymous web browsing environment. It's important that servers are able to run within the I2P environment, as outbound proxies to the normal Internet might be monitored, taken down, or taken over as malicious attacks are attempted.

WHY WOULD LIBRARIES OFFER THE DARK WEB?

The American Library Association encourages libraries to "install the Tor browser on public computers as a privacy option for users."[42] But why? What value does the Tor browser offer that other services do not? In the prior chapter, we discussed the privacy that VPNs can provide; why would we waste our time with the dark web? For one thing, it is really easy to use. The terminology involved with the dark web, and the concepts behind how it works, seems complex, but from the perspective of the user interface the Tor Browser is no more difficult to use than a traditional web browser. It is itself just a browser, created using a Firefox shell (so it very much has the look and feel of Firefox).

It is also super secure, owing to the networking principles used by the system. Imagine setting up a system where you send a message and it gets encrypted—or placed in a secure lockbox—and then sent to another person. This person places the message within another lockbox and then sends the message to another person known only by them, who adds another layer of protection and sends it to another person only they know. And this continues so on and on until the message reaches the intended recipient, who is able to unlock the boxes and retrieve the message. This is a lot more secure than traditional web access, which is more like putting a message on a chalkboard and hoping no one other than the intended recipient sees it. So we have convenience, we have privacy and security . . . and we have cost. Tor is completely free. It is a perfectly practical solution for libraries.

That said, the dark web comes with a few policy challenges that libraries would need to address. Given its harmful history—associated with now-defunct sites like the Silk Road, which allowed for the sale of illicit drugs and weapons—there needs to be some justification for use of the platform as well as a policy for its policing. While it may not be necessary to mention this point on the library's website (it would just invite controversy), it is good to be aware and have a response should the matter be raised (as it was in the first few libraries that offered the Tor platform).

As for policing Tor use among library patrons, might it be possible to balance online privacy with the need of the library to ensure that no illegal content is accessed? Unlike the other concepts in this book, this is an issue with essentially no precedent, but it is one that many libraries will likely demand be answered before they will consider offering Tor. Here are a few suggestions for policy. In any case, the policy that the library decides on should be made absolutely clear.

1. For the "very conservative" library: Have special computer stations that are Tor enabled. As many libraries do with removing Internet filtering for bona fide requests, allow only adults to use these computers, and caution users that web activity may be monitored by library employees but will remain private among the employees unless illegal activity is detected.

   • This is not the suggested approach. We think it is better to have trust in your patrons to make appropriate decisions. However, if it is either do this or not offer access at all, then do this!

2. The "leans conservative" approach: Have special computer stations that are Tor enabled that adult users may utilize for bona fide reasons if they have concerns about their online privacy. No monitoring of activity by library employees.

3. The "moderate" approach: Offer Tor on all "adult" computers. Do not proactively market the browser, necessarily, but ensure that all users are aware that it is an option for them to use.

4. The "liberal" approach: Make Tor available on all adult-use computers. Have a policy of promoting the browser to users as a way to enhance their online privacy.

Those few libraries that do offer Tor, at the time of this book's writing, mostly just offer it as another browser option (i.e., the "moderate" approach). These tend to be a bit more progressive libraries, with leadership that is fairly tech-savvy or proactive about privacy issues. As this privacy technology is adopted by more libraries, there is likely to be more variance in how it is adapted, like with the policy examples above.

A couple of disclaimers you may wish to include when providing access to the dark web:

•   The dark web offers enhanced privacy and security when using the web. It is not, however, infallible. There are always risks online, particularly when you share personal information with others. Exercise caution online—especially when using public computers.

•   Access to the dark web is unfiltered; however, the viewing of illicit materials /images on the web is still not permitted within the library. Those found to violate this policy will be permanently barred from future use of the library's computers.

•   The library and its systems collect local data about its users. Complete privacy cannot be offered. However, we take all possible steps to ensure that patron data remains private and secure.

•   Library staff is happy to assist you if you have any questions about this platform and how to use it.

•   This statement might also include links to information about Tor (like to the Tor Project website—https://torproject.org).

While adoption of dark web technologies is a new area with little precedent in library policy, we have done our best here to piece together our recommendations based on our knowledge of the platform. As you learn more about the platform and its benefits, and consider its use within the context of your library, you may wish to modify our suggestions to suit the needs of your library. This section, however, should provide a solid foundation for your policy efforts.

CONCLUSION

The dark web gets its name from the privacy it offers, but many still associate it with the illegal activity that has existed on the platform. This makes it valuable but also controversial. While the dark web has not been adopted by enough libraries to really get a strong idea of how policy will manifest, we have used our own background and knowledge of platforms like Tor to offer some suggestions on how you might develop a policy that suits the needs and sensibilities of your library. Hopefully, you can use the knowledge you have gained from this chapter, along with the suggestions we provide, to support the adoption of Tor for your public access computers.

NOTES

1. University of Groningen, *The postwar economy: 1945–1960*, retrieved December 18, 2019. http://www.let.rug.nl/usa/outlines/history-1994/postwar-america/the-postwar-economy-1945-1960.php

2. Tas Anjarwalla, "Inventor of cell phone: We knew someday everybody would have one," CNN, retrieved January 14, 2020. http://www.cnn.com/2010/TECH/mobile/07/09/cooper.cell.phone.inventor/index.html

3. Evan Andrews, *Who invented the internet? History stories*, updated October 28, 2019. https://www.history.com/news/who-invented-the-internet

4. Steel in the Air, *Wireless telecommunications timeline: 1983–present* (2014). https://www.steelintheair.com/wireless-industry-timeline

5. Adam Pothitos, *The history of the smartphone*, Mobile Industry Review (October 31, 2016). http://www.mobileindustryreview.com/2016/10/the-history-of-the-smartphone.html

6. L. Annaei Senecae, *Epistularum moralium ad lucilum liber sextus*, retrieved November 18, 2019. http://www.thelatinlibrary.com/sen/seneca.ep6.shtml

7. Pew Research Center, *A third of Americans live in a household with three or more smartphones*, retrieved May 25, 2017. https://www.pewresearch.org/fact-tank/2017/05/25/a-third-of-americans-live-in-a-household-with-three-or-more-smartphones

8. Pew Research, *A third of Americans*.

9. Oxford English Dictionary, 3rd ed., s.v. "internet, internet of things," retrieved January 6, 2020. https://www.oed.com/view/Entry/248411?redirectedFrom=internet+of+things#eid1191443070

10. Gilad Rosner and Erin Kenneally, *Privacy and the internet of things: Emerging frameworks for policy and design*, Center for Long-Term Cybersecurity (Berkeley, CA: UC Berkeley, June 7, 2018). https://papers.ssrn.com/sol3/papers.cfm?abstract_id=3320670

11. American Library Association, *Privacy: An interpretation of the Library Bill of Rights*, updated June 24, 2019. http://www.ala.org/advocacy/intfreedom/librarybill/interpretations/privacy

12. National Information Standards Organization, *NISO consensus principles on user's digital privacy in library, publisher, and software-provider systems*

(Baltimore, MD: Author, December 10, 2015). https://groups.niso.org/apps /group_public/download.php/16064/NISO%2520Privacy%2520Principles.pdf

13. Marshall Breeding, "Key technologies with implications for privacy," *Library Technology Reports* 55, no. 7 (October 2019): 5–19.

14. Google, *Secure your site with HTTPS: Protect your site and your users*, retrieved January 14, 2020. https://support.google.com/webmasters/answer /6073543?hl=en

15. Breeding, "Key technologies."

16. Let's Encrypt, *Home page*, retrieved January 14, 2020. https://letsencrypt .org/

17. Breeding, "Key technologies," p. 9.

18. Breeding, "Key technologies."

19. Dictionary.com, "deep web," retrieved October 28, 2019. https://www .dictionary.com/browse/deep-web?s=t

20. INFOSEC, *What is the difference between the surface web, the deep web, and the dark web?*, retrieved May 31, 2018. https://resources.infosecinstitute.com /what-is-the-difference-between-the-surface-web-the-deep-web-and-the-dark -web/#gref

21. Internet Live Stats, *Twitter usage statistics*, retrieved September 6, 2019. https://www.internetlivestats.com/twitter-statistics/

22. Robert W. Gehl, *Weaving the dark web: Legitimacy on Freenet, Tor, and I2P* (Cambridge, MA: The MIT Press, 2018).

23. Symantec Corporation, *How to safely access the deep and dark webs*, retrieved September 12, 2019. https://us.norton.com/internetsecurity-how-to -how-can-i-access-the-deep-web.html

24. Violet Blue, *The myth of Mariana's Web, the darkest corner of the inter- net. B@d P@ssw0rd*, retrieved December 1, 2019. https://www.engadget .com/2015/12/18/the-myth-of-marianas-web-the-darkest-corner-of-the-internet/

25. U.S. Defense Advanced Research Projects Agency, *Click farm, Adbusters* 23, no. 2 (March/April 2015): 52–73.

26. Adbusters, *Manifest*," retrieved September 12, 2019. http://abillionpeople .org/manifesto/

27. Don Patterson, *Dark web: A cheat sheet for business professionals*, *TechRepublic*, retrieved October 26, 2018. https://www.techrepublic.com/article /dark-web-the-smart-persons-guide/

28. Tim Fisher, *What is the dark web and why do people use it?*, *Lifewire*, revised July 19, 2019. https://web.archive.org/web/20200709115714

29. Tor, *About Tor: Overview*, retrieved September 12, 2019. https://2019.www .torproject.org/about/overview.html.en

30. Darren Guccione, *What is the dark web? How to access it and what you'll find*, CSO, updated March 5, 2020. https://www.csoonline.com/article/3249765 /what-is-the-dark-web-how-to-access-it-and-what-youll-find.html

31. Tor, *About Tor: Overview.*

32. Keith Kirkpatrick (2017). "Financing the dark web," *Society* 60, no. 3 (February 2017): 21–22. https://doi.org/10.1145/3037386

33. Julia Weber and Edwin W. Kruisbergen, "Criminal markets: The dark web, money laundering and counterstrategies—An overview of the 10th Research Conference on Organized Crime," *Trends in Organized Crime* 22, no. 3 (April 26, 2019): 346–356. https://doi.org/10.1007/s12117-019-09365-8

34. Fiammetta Piazza, "Bitcoin in the dark web: A shadow over banking secrecy and a call for global response. *Southern California Interdisciplinary Law Journal* 26, no. 3 (Summer 2017): 521.

35. Ibid.

36. Tor, *About Tor: Overview.*

37. Eric P. Delozier, "Anonymity and authenticity in the cloud: Issues and applications," *OCLC Systems & Services: International Digital Library Perspectives* 29, no. 2 (May 2013): 65–77.

38. Ibid.

39. Guardian Project, *Orbot: Proxy with Tor,* retrieved January 14, 2020. https://guardianproject.info/apps/orbot/

40. I2P, *Garlic routing and "garlic" terminology,* retrieved October 22, 2019. https://geti2p.net/en/docs/how/garlic-routing

41. I2P, *A gentle introduction to how I2P works,* retrieved October 22, 2019. https://geti2p.net/en/docs/how/intro

42. American Library Association, *Library privacy checklist for public access computers and networks,* updated January 26, 2020. http://www.ala.org/advocacy/privacy/checklists/public-access-computer

Glossary

ALA Core Values—The American Library Association created a set of core values that define, inform, and guide librarians in the practice of working in libraries. The core values are: Access, confidentiality or privacy, democracy, diversity, education and lifelong learning, intellectual freedom, public good, preservation, professionalism, service, social responsibility, and sustainability.

Blockchain—A blockchain is a series of data blocks connected by encrypted connections. Each block contains the decryption information for the previous block and the connection information to the next block.

Children's Internet Protection Act (CIPA)—One of several bills passed by the U.S. Congress to protect children from accessing pornography on the Internet. It requires that any school or library that accepts E-rate funds must have adequate Internet filtering installed.

Cookies (or HTTP cookie)—Cookies are small files of information that are sent by Internet sites to computers. They typically contain transactional data and activity. Cookies also can contain personally identifiable information and private information.

Dark web—The dark web is a part of the regular Internet that is not accessible without using specialized software like Tor. It is also not indexed by search engines.

E-rate—The E-rate program was created in 1997 and is run by the Federal Communications Commission. It provides discounts for telecommunications, Internet access, and internal connections to schools and libraries.

Evidence-based practice—Evidence-based practice is the process of identifying, retrieving, and using appropriate literature from various sources in health-care decisions.

Family Educational Rights and Privacy Act (FERPA)—FERPA is a federal law that determines who has access to educational information by some entities including employers, public institutions, and foreign governments.

Fingerprinting or digital fingerprinting—A set of information about a device or person on the Internet that when combined can be used to identify a specific device or person.

Health Insurance Portability and Accountability Act (HIPAA)—Passed by Congress in 1996, the HIPAA act modernizes the way that health information is stored, accessed, and secured. It protects personally identifiable information from being used in manners inconsistent with health care.

HTTPS (HyperText Transfer Protocol Secure)—Hypertext Transfer Protocol is the language that Internet sites use to transfer websites. It is secure if it is using a protected connection that prevents intrusion.

Information ethics—Information ethics is the focus on the idea that the creation, organization, dissemination, and use of information abides by the same ethical standards and moral codes that are used in society.

Information privacy—Information privacy is the idea that personally identifiable information should be stored in ways that keep it private.

Library policy—Libraries operate based on policies set by their boards or committees. Policies define the way the library operates in conjunction with local, state, and federal law.

The Onion Router—see Tor.

Personally identifiable information (PII)—Personally identifiable information are pieces of information that when used alone or with other relevant data can be used to identify an individual. Some examples of PII include direct identifiers like driver's license or passport information, or more indirect identifiers like date of birth.

Tor (previously known as The Onion Router)—Tor is a specialized Internet browser that is used to browse the regular Internet using a specialized network that works to provide anonymity. It is also used to connect to a part of the dark web.

USA PATRIOT Act—The USA PATRIOT Act was an act of the U.S. Congress that was signed into law by President George W. Bush on October 26, 2001. The act was designed in response to the 2001 September 11 attacks on the World Trade Center and the anthrax attacks of 2001. The act has been criticized for infringing on the civil rights of Americans.

Additional Resources

The purpose of this chapter is to provide a list of resources that, while not discussed at length in the book, provide useful information about these topics.

CHAPTER ONE

A few resources are interesting to read for a historical perspective on the topic of patron relations and privacy, though their modern relevance may be somewhat limited.

Daniel Fidel Ferrer, "Try today's hip technology: Portable flash drives," *Computers in Libraries* 23, no. 10 (2003): 63–64.

Aimee Fifarek, "Technology and privacy in the academic library," *Online Information Review* 26, no. 6 (2002): 366–374.

Bonnie L. Turner and Rondi Downs, *Patron relations: A survival manual* (Yakima, WA: Yakima Valley Regional Library, 1983).

These resources look at different yet related aspects of patron privacy. The first looks at what library vendors are doing to preserve privacy. The second is a scoping, introductory look at general privacy topics:

Lori Bowen Ayre, "Protecting patron privacy: Vendors, libraries, and patrons each have a role to play," *Collaborative Librarianship* 9, no. 1 (2017): Article 2.

Bobbi Newman and Bonnie Tijerina, *Protecting patron privacy: A LITA guide* (Lanham, MD: Rowman & Littlefield, 2017).

CHAPTER TWO

Nicholson and Smith offer an interesting perspective on library privacy based on HIPAA privacy policies:

Scott Nicholson and Catherine Arnott Smith, "Using lessons from health care to protect the privacy of library users: Guidelines for the de-identification of library data based on HIPAA," *Journal of the Association for Information Science and Technology* 58, no. 8 (2007): 1198–1206.

Articles that discuss library patron data privacy are quite numerous and have emerged over a long period of time. The articles selected here give a strong longitudinal overview of the development of this topic:

Rhoda Garoogian, "Librarian/patron confidentiality: An ethical challenge," *Library Trends* 40, no. 2 (1991): 216–233.

Anne Klinefelter, "Privacy and library public services: Or, I know what you read last summer," *Legal Reference Services Quarterly* 26, no. 1/2 (2007): 253–279.

Angela C. Million and Kim N. Fisher, "Library records: A review of confidentiality laws and practices," *Journal of Academic Librarianship* 11, no. 6 (1986): 346–349.

Younghee Noh, "A study on developing and proposing the library privacy policy," *Journal of the Korean Society for Library and Information Science* 46, no. 4 (2012): 207–242 (text in Korean).

Ann M. Snowman, "Privacy and confidentiality: Using scenarios to teach your staff about patrons' rights," *Journal of Access Services* 10, no. 2 (2013): 120–132.

Paul Sturges, Eric Davies, James Dearnley, Ursula Iliffe, Charles Oppenheim, and Rachel Hardy, "User privacy in the digital library environment: An investigation of policies and preparedness," *Library Management* 24, no. 1/2 (2003): 44–50.

CHAPTER THREE

Disruptive patron behavior in libraries (some older resources):

Frank J. DeRosa, "The disruptive patron," *Library and Archival Security* 3, no. 3/4 (1982): 29–37.

Barbara Pease, "Workplace violence in libraries," *Library Management* 16, no. 7 (1995): 30–39.

Photography and library social media use resources:

Stephanie Johnson, *Visitor photography policy: An exploration of current trends and considerations across American museums* (master's thesis). University of Oregon, 2014. https://scholarsbank.uoregon.edu/xmlui/handle/1794/17940

Bryce C. Newell and David P. Randall, *Video surveillance in public libraries: A case of unintended consequences?*, 46th Hawaii International Conference on System Sciences, 2013. https://doi.org/10.1109/HICSS.2013.595

Troy A. Swanson, *Managing social media in libraries: Finding collaboration, coordination, and focus* (Oxford, UK: Chanos Publishing, 2012).

Samuel D. Warren and Louis D. Brandeis, "Privacy, photography, and the press," *Harvard Law Review* 111, no. 4 (1998): 1086–1103.

Martin Zimmerman, "Technology and privacy erosion in United States libraries: A personal viewpoint," *New Library World* 111, no. 1/2 (2010): 7–15.

CHAPTER FOUR

Crime and violence in libraries:

Sarah Farrugia, "A dangerous occupation? Violence in public libraries," *New Library World* 103, no. 9 (2002): 309–319.

Alan J. Lincoln and Carol Z. Lincoln, "The impact of crime in public libraries," *Library and Archival Security* 3, no. 3/4 (1982): 125–137.

Hannah McGrath and Anne Goulding, "Part of the job: Violence in public libraries," *New Library World* 97, no. 3 (1996): 4–13.

Rhea J. Rubin, *Defusing the angry patron* (Chicago, IL: Neal Schuman Publishers, 2010).

Police intervention in libraries:

Sheila Burnette, "Book 'em! Cops and librarians working together," *American Libraries* 29, no. 2 (1998): 48–50.

Stephen Cresswell, "The last days of Jim Crow in southern libraries," *Libraries and Culture* 31, no. 3/4 (1996): 557–573.

Bryce C. Newell and David P. Randall, "Video surveillance in public libraries: A case of unintended consequences?" In the *Proceedings of the 2013 Hawaii International Conference on System Sciences* (New York, NY: Institute of Electrical and Electronics Engineers): 1932–1941.

Michele Reutty, "What happened to me when the police came knocking," *Computers in Libraries* 27, no. 6 (2007): 11–12.

CHAPTER FIVE

Library patron computer privacy tips:

Howard Carter, "Misuse of library public access computers: Balancing privacy, accountability, and security," *Journal of Library Administration* 36, no. 4 (2002): 29–48.

Christine Dettlaff, "Protecting user privacy in the library," *Community and Junior College Libraries* 13, no. 4 (2007): 7–8.

Steven Johns and Karen Lawson, "University undergraduate students and library-related privacy issues," *Library and Information Science Research* 27, no. 4 (2005): 485–495.

These resources discuss the emergence of patron privacy as a core value for librarianship and a valued attribute of library services:

Howard Falk, "Privacy in libraries," *Electronic Library* 22, no. 3 (2004): 281–284.

Nikki Tummon and Dawn McKinnon, "Attitudes and practices of Canadian academic librarians regarding library and online privacy: A national study," *Library and Information Science Research* 40, no. 2 (2018): 86–97.

Steve Witt, "The evolution of privacy within the American Library Association, 1906–2002." *Library Trends* 65, no. 4 (2017): 639–657.

Jeannette Woodward, *What every librarian should know about electronic privacy* (Westport, CT: Libraries Unlimited, 2007).

CHAPTER SIX

These are a few resources that challenge conceptions of what libraries are and should be, including whether a library can exist outside of the physical building:

Michael Buckland, *Redesigning library services: A manifesto* (Chicago, IL: American Library Association, 1992).

Geoffrey Freeman, Scott Bennett, Sam Demas, Bernard Frischer, Christina Peterson, and Kathleen Oliver, *Library as place: Rethinking roles, rethinking space* (Washington, DC: Council on Library and Information Resources, 2005).

Marion Wilson, "Understanding the needs of tomorrow's library user: Rethinking library services for the new age," *Australasian Public Libraries and Information Services* 13, no. 2 (2000): 81–86.

Resources for keeping patrons secure when accessing library content remotely:

Joseph A. Cazier and B. Dawn Medlin, "Password security: An empirical investigation into e-commerce passwords and their crack times," *Information Systems Security* 15, no. 6 (2006): 45–55.

Rosemarie Cooper, Paula R. Dempsey, Vanaja Menon, and Christopher Millson-Martula, "Remote library users: Needs and expectations," *Library Trends* 47, no. 1 (1998): 42–64.

Donnelyn Curtis, *Attracting, educating, and serving remote users through the web: A how-to-do-it manual for librarians* (London, UK: Facet Publishing, 2002).

Terry Henner, "Bridging the distance: Bibliographic instruction for remote library users," *Medical Reference Services Quarterly* 21, no. 1 (2002): 79–85.

Tom N. Jagatic, Nathaniel A. Johnson, Markus Jakobsson, and Filippo Menczer, "Social phishing," *Communications of the Association for Computing Machinery* 50, no. 10 (2007): 94–100. https://dl.acm.org/doi/fullHtml/10.1145/1290958.1290968

Lesley M. Moyo and Ellysa S. Cahoy. "Meeting the needs of remote library users," *Library Management* 24, no. 6/7 (2003): 281–290.

Paul Tremblay and Zhonghong Wang, "We care—virtually and in person: A user-centered approach to assessment, implementation and promotion of library resources and services to a remote graduate campus," *Public Services Quarterly* 4, no. 3 (2008): 207–232.

Rick Walsh and Emilee Rader, "Understanding password choices: How frequently entered passwords are re-used across websites," *Proceedings of the 12th Symposium on Usable Privacy and Security* (2016). https://www.usenix.org/system/files/conference/soups2016/soups2016-paper-wash.pdf

CHAPTER SEVEN

In our scenario this chapter, the topic of fake news arises. Although its discussion is not within the scope of this book on privacy, the issue is currently an important one. These resources speak to news access and trustworthiness, and many contain links to other resources of interest:

Sarah McCammon, "Troll watch: Study shows older Americans share the most fake news," interview with Andy Guess, Princeton University, *National Public Radio: All Things Considered* (January 13, 2019). https://www.npr.org/2019/01/13/684994772/troll-watch-study-shows-older-americans-share-the-most-fake-news

Amy Mitchell, Jeffrey Gottfried, Galen Stocking, Mason Walker, and Sophia Fedeli, "Many Americans say made-up news is a critical problem that needs to be fixed," Pew Research Center, retrieved June 5, 2019. https://www.journalism.org/2019/06/05/many-americans-say-made-up-news-is-a-critical-problem-that-needs-to-be-fixed

Elisa Shearer, "Social media outpaces print newspapers in the U.S. as a news source," Pew Research Center Fact Tank, retrieved December 10, 2018. https://www .pewresearch.org/fact-tank/2018/12/10/social-media-outpaces-print-newspapers -in-the-u-s-as-a-news-source

The chapter also touches on the history of the Internet and the World Wide Web. These resources can aid in your understanding of the topics:

World Wide Web Consortium (W3C; https://www.w3.org/) is led by Tim Berners-Lee and Jeffrey Jaffe. Its mission is to "lead the web to its full potential." Within the consortium, several pages may be of interest (all pages retrieved April 23, 2020):

- HTML and CSS: https://www.w3.org/standards/webdesign/htmlcss
- Audio and Video: https://www.w3.org/standards/webdesign/audiovideo
- Privacy: https://www.w3.org/standards/webdesign/privacy
- Accessibility (including updated Web Content Accessibility Guidelines): https://www.w3.org/standards/webdesign/accessibility
- Mobile Web: https://www.w3.org/standards/webdesign/mobilweb

A printable handout from Homeland Security can be found at the site below:

U.S. Department of Homeland Security (flyer), "Social media bots overview" (May 2018). https://www.cisa.gov/sites/default/files/publications/19_0717_cisa_social-media -bots-overview.pdf

Clifford Colby and Rae Hodge, "Best password manager to use for 2021: 1Password, LastPass and more compared," CNet, retrieved March 17, 2021. https://www .cnet.com/news/best-password-managers-for-2020/. This comparison can be helpful as you choose between features and prices for various password managers.

CHAPTER EIGHT

Marshall Breeding, creator and editor of *Library Technology Guides* (https:// librarytechnology.org), is a recognized expert in the field of integrated library systems and library technologies. These chapters provide good information for any library, and are available via print book, as well as the periodical that originally published these chapters:

Marshall Breeding, *Protecting privacy on library websites: Critical technologies and implementation trends* (Chicago, IL: ALA TechSource, 2019).
Marshall Breeding, "Protecting privacy on library websites: Critical technologies and implementation trends," *Library Technology Reports* 55, no. 3 (October 2019).

The Federal Trade Commission offers advice on the use of public networks, and also links readers to privacy for individuals' home wireless networks:

Federal Trade Commission Consumer Information, "Tips for using public Wi-Fi networks," updated March 2014. https://www.consumer.ftc.gov/articles/0014-tips -using-public-wi-fi-networks

These articles discuss patron education and behavior from a technology perspective:

T. J. Lamanna, "On educating patrons on privacy and maximizing library resources," *Information Technology and Libraries* 38, no. 3 (September 2019): 4–7.

France Belanger and Robert E. Crossler, "Dealing with digital traces: Understanding protective behaviors on mobile devices," *Journal of Strategic Information Systems* 28, no. 1 (November 2018): 34–49. https://doi.org/10.1016/j.jsis.2018.11.002

Edward M. Corrado, "Libraries and protecting patron privacy," *Technical Services Quarterly* 37, no. 1: 44–54. https://doi.org/10.1080/07317131.2019.1691761

This study examines actual behaviors of adults who are asked to provide personal information. The insights here can be helpful as librarians work to understand patron information seeking as it relates to privacy tolerance:

Patricia A. Norberg, Daniel R. Horne, and David A. Horne, "The privacy paradox: Personal information disclosure intentions versus behaviors," *Journal of Consumer Affairs* 41, no. 1 (Summer 2007): 100–126.

Finally, these resources discuss young adults and social media practices:

Paige Alfonzo, *Mastering mobile through social media: Creating engaging content on Instagram and Snapchat* (Chicago, IL: ALA TechSource, 2019).

Rachel M. Magee, Margaret H. Buck, Juliana Kitzmann, Nathaniel Morris, Dylan Petrimoulx, Matthew Rich, Joshua Sensiba, Eyan Tiemann, and Aiden Wempe, "Teen social media practice and perceptions of peers: Implications for youth services providers and researchers," *Journal of Research on Libraries and Young Adults* 10, no. 3 (November 2019). http://www.yalsa.ala.org/jrlya/wp-content/uploads/2019/11/Magee_TeenSocialMediaPerceptions_FINAL.pdf

CHAPTER NINE

The Internet of Things (IoT) relates more to home life than libraries (at least currently), but like other technologies offers risk and rewards for use. These resources explore that realm:

American Library Association, *Libraries and the IoT*, retrieved April 23, 2020. http://www.ala.org/tools/librariestransform/future/blog/fri-05122017-0844

Gilad Rosner and Erin Kenneally, *Privacy and the internet of things: Emerging frameworks for policy and design* (Berkeley, CA: UC Berkeley Center for Long-Term Cybersecurity, 2018).

Elham Ali Shammar and Ammar Thabit Zahary, "The internet of things (IoT): A survey of techniques, operating systems, and trends," *Library Hi Tech* 38, no. 1 (October 5, 2019): 5–66.

Felicia Yusuf, Goodluck Ifijeh, and Sola Owolabi, "Awareness of internet of things and its potential in enhancing academic library service delivery in a developing country," *Library Philosophy and Practice* (September 2019). https://digitalcommons.unl.edu/cgi/viewcontent.cgi?article=6282&context=libphilprac

To explore current Bitcoin topics, navigate to Investor.gov, ICOs, and Digital Assets:

Damian S. Damianov and Ahmed H. Elsayed, "Does Bitcoin add value to global industry portfolios?" *Economics Letters* (December 2019). https://www.researchgate.net/profile/Damian_Damianov/publication/338408733_Does_Bitcoin_add_value_to_global_industry_portfolios/links/5e60b62e299bf1bdb85440bf/Does-Bitcoin-add-value-to-global-industry-portfolios.pdf

Investor.gov. https://www.investor.gov/additional-resources/spotlight/spotlight-initial-coin-offerings -and-digital-assets

Considering the dark web and its uses for libraries:

Matt Beckstrom and Brady Lund, *Casting light on the dark web: A guide for safe exploration* (Lanham, MD: Rowman & Littlefield, 2019).

Brady Lund and Matt Beckstrom, "The integration of Tor into library services: An appeal to the core mission and values of libraries," *Public Library Quarterly* (November 19, 2019). https://doi.org/10.1080/01616846.2019.1696078

Carrie Smith, "In the deep beneath the iceberg: Understanding the dark web and internet privacy," *American Libraries* (June 24, 2019). https://americanlibrariesmagazine .org/blogs/the-scoop/deep-beneath-iceberg/

Index

About the Authors

MATTHEW A. BECKSTROM was born and raised in Montana. He has been with the Lewis & Clark Library in Helena, Montana, since 1999 as the systems manager/librarian. Beckstrom also teaches management and technology courses at the University of Montana-Helena College. He received his undergraduate degree in computer science from Montana State University Billings in 2010 and graduated with his master's of information science in information systems degree from the University of North Texas in 2012. He has written and contributed to several books on privacy, security, and the Internet. He is also a frequent presenter at conferences on a variety of topics including technology, security, and privacy. For more information on his upcoming publications and presentations, visit matthewbeckstrom.com.

BRADY D. LUND is a doctoral student at Emporia State University's School of Library and Information Management. He is coauthor, along with Matt Beckstrom, of the 2019 book *Casting Light on the Dark Web: A Guide for Safe Exploration*. He has published several peer-reviewed journal articles on the topics of information technology and information privacy and is a regular presenter on these topics at regional and national conferences.

SANDRA J. VALENTI is an assistant professor in the School of Library and Information Management at Emporia State University, where she earned her PhD in library and information science and a master's degree in instructional design and technology. A previous stint in the business world informs her work on the basis of years of people and operations management. Current interests include virtual communities of practice, the ACRL roles and strengths and how libraries use them for information literacy instruction, and the preparation of librarians for their upcoming professional roles.